Somebody's Darling

Somebody's Darling

Essays on the Civil War

KENT GRAMM

INDIANA
University Press

Bloomington & Indianapolis

This book is a publication of

Indiana University Press

601 North Morton Street

Bloomington, IN 47404-3797 USA

http://iupress.indiana.edu

Telephone orders 800-842-6796

Fax orders 812-855-7931

Orders by e-mail iuporder@indiana.edu

© 2002 by Kent Gramm

The paper used in this publication meets the minimum requirements of American National Standard for Information Sciences — Permanence of Paper for Printed Library Materials, ANSI Z39.48-1984.

Manufactured in the United States of America

Library of Congress Cataloging-in-Publication Data

Gramm, Kent.

Somebody's darling : essays on the Civil War / Kent Gramm.

p. cm.

Includes bibliographical references and index.

ISBN 0-253-34081-0 (alk. paper)

1. United States — History — Civil War, 1861–1865 — Influence. 2. United States — History — Civil War, 1861–1865 — Social aspects. 3. United States — History — Civil War, 1861–1865 — Literature and the war. 4. Gettysburg (Pa.), Battle of, 1863. 5. Wilderness, Battle of the, Va., 1864. I. Title.

E468.9 .G74 2002

973.7 — dc21

2001006085

1   2   3   4   5   07   06   05   04   03   02

For Somebody's Darlings
and for Alan Nolan

Into the ward of the clean white-wash'd halls,
　Where the dead slept and the dying lay;
　Wounded by bayonets, sabres, and balls,
　Somebody's darling was borne one day.
Somebody's darling, so young and so brave,
Wearing still on his sweet, yet pale face —
　Soon to be hid in the dust of the grave,
The lingering light of his boyhood's grace.
　Somebody's darling, somebody's pride.
Who'll tell his mother where her boy died?

Give him a kiss but for somebody's sake,
　Murmur a prayer for him soft and low;
One little curl from its golden mates take,
　Somebody's pride it was once you know;
Somebody's warm hand has oft rested there,
　Was it a mother's, so soft and white?
　Or have the lips of a sister so fair
Ever been bath'd in their waves of light?
Somebody's darling, somebody's pride,
Who'll tell his mother where her boy died?
　— "Somebody's Darling," 1864

My subject is war, and the pity of war.
　— Wilfred Owen

CONTENTS

CONTENTS

Introduction:
What Was It Like?

Broader and deeper we must write our annals.
— Emerson, "History"

This book is for any reader who thinks about life; yet the essays are all related some way or other to the American Civil War. You will not find tactical studies of battles here, although there are a few battle narratives. The Civil War buff will notice chapter titles relating to Gettysburg and the Wilderness, but might wonder what either of these has to do with the poetry of Keats or a novel by a twentieth century Icelander.

The inspiration for this book is a song whose lyrics were written by a Southern woman in 1864. What did she — a sentimental young lady who wrote verses — know about the Civil War? More than we ever will. Consequently, this book is quite sympathetic to songs and poetry and other arts. The implication throughout these pages is that traditional Civil War studies have missed some important things. Once we broaden our interests, we not only discover things about the Civil War, we find that war can teach us a few things about life.

Reader, I hope the Civil War becomes your Walden. For Henry David Thoreau, the pond in Massachusetts became a window to life. Do not worry that the idea has been used up: the Civil War was bigger than Walden Pond, and at least as deep. So if *Walden* is a book about a pond, this is a book about a war.

(If you are not a Civil War nut, I suggest that you stop reading right here and proceed to the first essay, "The Gettysburg Nobody Knows.")

This is also a book for anyone who loves the Civil War. And some of us do love it, to admit it frankly. Presumably we are not sociopathic maniacs. Many of us — probably most of us — abhor war. Yet we love this one. And "love" is not too strong a word. We pretty much give ourselves to this war. We spend not only our leisure on it, but also all our spare change. And we think about it all the time, even when we are with someone else. You might even say that the Civil War itself is somebody's darling: ours.

What exactly do we love? Not the killing, not the more than six hundred thousand burials; not the grief suffered across the nation in homes mourning fathers and husbands, friends and brothers. For truly, somebody's darlings — to the tune of 5 million in terms of today's population — lie buried in small graves. I suspect that we do not really love the excitement and spectacle of the war, though such things — again, speaking frankly — have interested and entertained people since the Trojan War and before. Warfare can be exhilarating, challenging, character building, and all that. Nevertheless, the Civil War was not a football season and I think most of us know it. Most of us would gladly give up our books and our reenactments if it would mean that 625,000 sons, brothers, fathers, and husbands could be restored to their loved ones. For many who study the War have learned a little about honor and unselfishness from those nineteenth-century Americans.

Not that we could honestly want the War entirely undone, for it made our country and us what we are. Nor could we easily abandon the people we have come to know and admire. We would not want Abraham Lincoln wiped out of our memory, nor Robert E. Lee, U. S. Grant, Stuart, Sherman, Stonewall Jackson, Joshua Chamberlain, or those many humble Yanks and Rebs whose letters we read and whose patient, courageous footsteps we trace. They have become *our* darlings, in a good sense. Many a modern eye becomes moist at their graves. Many a contemporary heart is lifted at the thought of what they did and said. We would be bereft without them, as their families were.

But history and our neighborhoods are full of interesting people to know and admire, so I doubt that we love the Civil War only because of the people we have come to know in the books. Our attachment to the War began long before we read about the Blue and the Gray.

Something started us on the War. That same something did not start other people. We visited a Civil War battlefield; so did people who never caught fire. We go back to the battlefields, but they do not. We saw a television program on the Civil War and were surprised at how interested in it we became. Two hundred million people watch television, but 200 million people did not become buffs. We had an ancestor in the War; so did 50 million other Americans. We love the War because of something that was in us before battlefields, books, television, movies, or ancestors.

Those of us who read about the War like our tactical studies and biographies. Such books always sell, let critics say what they might — with justification — about how the same thing gets published over and over again. As for myself, I confess that I would rather settle down with some new book on the Battle of the Wilderness than do almost anything else — except visit the Wilderness. But if I were offered a two-minute visit back in time to May 1864 on the Tapp Farm without getting killed for my curiosity, I would drop my book in an instant. Most of us would. Some of us would even risk the getting killed.

So we do not love the books or the facts for themselves. They are only substitutes. Substitutes for what? For the real thing. The books are not the real thing, nor are the battlefield tours. However close we come to the real thing now, we must get there in the imagination. The reason most of us would rather trade a great deal of Civil War study for two minutes in Lincoln's office or Lee's headquarters or in the Sunken Road is that we want to know *what it was like*. Although it is interesting to know that Hooker issued an attack order for 5 A.M., we begin to experience something when we read that the fighting in the Cornfield at Antietam was "like a tumbling-together of heaven and earth" — a statement which starts the imagination working. "So," we muse, "that's what it felt like."

Once we talk about what something was *like*, we have stepped outside the realm of History (capitalized to signify a subject matter, an academic field, a body of written work) — which is good, because the War itself took place outside of History. It took place in real life — with all its pains, visions, emotions, and strangeness. That is why Walt Whitman said, "the real war will never get in the books."

When another poet, Robert Burns, wrote "O my luv's like a red, red rose," he avoided quantitative facts, as well as abstractions like "beautiful," "fragrant," "passionate," and "sharp," because he wanted to say what the woman he loved was like. Oh yes, she is twenty-three, and she is beautiful; but she is like a rose. Like a red, red rose. Within decent limits, Burns wanted us to experience that young woman.

You may prove your love is beautiful with facts from A to Z,
but the Yellow Rose of Texas is the only girl for me.

Or in other words, a sunset is not the red glow from a fireplace; it is light waves converted to electrical impulses transmitted along neurons. But it is more like the glow of a fireplace than it is like "electrical impulses."*

It is human to try to understand life intellectually, because to understand intellectually means, in part, to control, even if the control is only over our own reactions. But when we intellectualize an experience, we restrict, order, arrange, and select reality — to produce something that works in our minds. That is why real life seldom makes sense. It does not operate under our restrictions. To understand the Civil War intellectually is one thing; it is a theoretical, political, moral, abstract thing. But to experience what it was like is another thing.

Of course, these essays are not the real thing. A book is only a book, including this one, and Civil War books are to the Civil War as Lincoln pennies are to Lincoln. But our imaginations can go beyond the pages. The writers I have called upon — Keats, Homer, Walt Whitman — open the shutters of the imagination; they understand life in ways that are not solely intellectual.

Fortunately, we are not accustomed to looking through those startlingly clear but dreamlike windowpanes to the past. Who wants to go through what those Americans went through during the Civil War?

We do. I expect that we are willing to be anything but comfortable. True, the history books can be comforting. When we are disturbed by something, we can often turn to a Civil War book to settle down. The Civil War can be a relief from the stresses of work and home. But of course, it is actually only Civil War *books* that are a relief: the War itself was infinitely worse than the stresses we usually complain about, and the soldiers would have given anything to be out of their place and in ours instead, if they could have done so without abandoning their causes. The War itself, as war, was "nothing but hell and lots of it." So the more we experience what the War was *like*, the more uncomfortable we should become, if we are not depraved. We should be uncomfortable that we love a war, and we should be uncomfortable whenever we catch a glimpse of it. But through the discomfort that accompanies the bliss of true love, we can become better than we were. We desire to be like them a little — those Somebody's Darlings whose lives and deaths were significant. In part, we are willing to share their discomforts because to share the Civil War generation's experiences might lend our own lives some of the meaning the War gave to theirs. So, like the most earnest of

---

*I flirted briefly with the idea of titling this introduction "Death by Poetry."

them, we are volunteers. We are volunteering to live and fight and suffer with them for a while.

The people and the times of the Civil War are related to us in some strong and personal way. Somebody's darling is involved in every war. Therefore we cannot, or ought not, love a war as war. "War is cruelty," Sherman said; "you cannot refine it." War is not like a championship football game; it is more like a shooting in a 7-11. The resemblance is not only in the action itself, but also in its consequences, which are virtually unspeakable.

So where does that put those of us who love this war? Some would say that our connection to the Civil War lies in our human nature, which loves to fight and kill. This unflattering characterization does not feel right, or at least it does not feel good; but I would be willing to accept it so long as it is not considered to be a complete portrait. Perhaps some men and women study war to keep up their courage, and others study it to face their fears. Perhaps some of us crave excitement, and perhaps some of us just want to figure things out. Be any of that as it may, I think there is another aspect to our love of the Civil War.

For many of us, revisiting the Civil War is like going home.

Somebody's Darling

> There are secret articles in our treaties with the gods,
> of more importance than all the rest, which the historian can never know.
> — THOREAU

The Gettysburg Nobody Knows

On the afternoon of Thursday, July 2, 1863, the second day at Gettysburg, Captain John Bigelow's 9th Massachusetts Battery was on a firing line where nobody should have been, let alone artillery unsupported by infantry. Major General Daniel Sickles had moved his 3d Corps out from the main Union line of battle along lower Cemetery Ridge, going forward to the Emmitsburg Road. One half of his corps, Brig. Gen. Andrew Humphreys's division, took position along the road; the other division, Maj. Gen. David Birney's, stretched back at an angle toward Little Round Top — though there were not enough men actually to extend the line back that far. Nor were there enough infantrymen for Birney to connect in an unbroken line with Humphreys's left. The division along the road ended several hundred yards short of a peach orchard where the Wheatfield Road intersected the Emmitsburg Road; Birney put one brigade in the orchard, but it was disconnected at both flanks — no infantry to the right or left.

The infantry could not cover the ground because Sickles had taken it upon himself to occupy a line longer by 50 percent than the one his corps had been assigned. He was supposed to occupy lower Cemetery Ridge and connect to Little Round Top, securing that hill. Probably thinking he could cover that line and its commanding hill by taking position forward of them, Sickles had become dissatisfied with his instructions. He remembered that two months earlier at Chancellorsville he had obeyed orders and left some high ground to the enemy, who had proceeded to place artillery upon it and blast the Union center to rags. Standing where Cemetery Hill petered out into low ground before rising toward Little Round Top, he looked to his front and saw that the Wheatfield-Emmitsburg Road intersection and its peach orchard were higher up than he was. Of course it was lower than Little Round Top and about a mile in front of the rest of the army, but Sickles was an amateur and he did not like taking orders, so he advanced his spotty mile-and-a-half line of troops.[1] Major General Winfield Scott Hancock of the 2d Corps, which had been connected to Sickles's right, watched the advance with wide eyes, wondering whether he had somehow failed to receive an order for the whole army to go forward. But no, he was merely witnessing yet another example of what Saint Augustine called *massa damnata*.

The term refers to the idea that everyone is a victim of everyone else's errors and bad behavior — "sin," the saint would have called it. In this case a brave, childish, incompetent officer (Dan Sickles) implicated not only his own corps, as it turned out, but a good part of both armies in a chaotic and inefficient bloodbath. Such is the story of military history, more or less, and as such it sheds light on human history in general, which is why some people study wars. Specifically and personally implicated in Sickles's unauthorized move was Lt. Christopher Erickson, an immigrant from Norway who had enlisted in the Union army for reasons nobody knows and found himself sitting on a horse, commanding a section (two guns) of Captain Bigelow's 9th Massachusetts Battery. It was a very bad place and time to be sitting on a horse. Because Sickles had too few men for the left half of his line, he stretched six artillery batteries, under the command of Lt. Col. Freeman McGilvery, between the intersection where Humphreys's infantry left off, and the wheatfield where Birney's infantry, except for the isolated brigade in the peach orchard, began. No Union infantry was in line to support Bigelow or the batteries between him and the orchard. Such positioning was virtually unheard-of in the Civil War because it was stupid or desperate. If there were no infantry to support a battery, enemy infantry could come forward and kill or wound the artillerymen and horses, then capture the guns and turn them around.

And here was a line of six exposed batteries, out in the open on the crest of an elevation. The leftmost was Bigelow's six guns, and mounted behind two of them sat Lieutenant Erickson. Sure enough, before this line had been in position more than a few minutes, they were hit. Lieutenant General James Longstreet's corps of the Army of Northern

Virginia was under orders to move out from a line of woods, cross the Emmitsburg Road, and attack what the Confederate high command thought was the exposed Union flank on lower Cemetery Ridge. Their direction of advance would bring thousands of Rebels right across the peach orchard, where instead of nothing stood a line of stalwart sitting ducks.

To repeat, one such duck was Christopher Erickson. Straight up the slope came two regiments and one battalion of Brig. Gen. Joseph Kershaw's brigade, and except for some confusion they would have rushed up through the shot and shell and captured all six batteries. But the Rebel line of battle had halted and moved by the right flank, everyone mistakenly obeying orders directed only to the far-right element.[2] It took time to realign the units, move them left, and wheel back toward the Wheatfield Road. Meanwhile, Confederate artillery had lit up in an arc starting from across the Emmitsburg Road, perpendicular to and even toward the rear of Bigelow's line, around toward their front. The Union batteries were caught in a cross fire. Then, as if to show that things can always get worse, the men in the Union division along the Emmitsburg Road (the right flank and rear of Bigelow et al.) began pulling back toward Cemetery Ridge. They did this because it was obvious that the unsupported artillery line perpendicular to their left could not stand a combined infantry-artillery assault. Humphreys's division would have been outflanked; they had no choice but to withdraw. So now Bigelow and the other batteries were outflanked. Not only was Kershaw's infantry commencing to attack in front, Brig. Gen. William Barksdale's Mississippi brigade was advancing across the Emmitsburg Road in pursuit of Humphreys, meaning that in a few minutes they would be directly in Bigelow's rear.

All of this might look rather orderly on a map, but in the actual event, that Union artillery position along upper Wheatfield Road was pandemonium. Not only were bullets flying, hitting horses and men, but Confederate shot and shells were plowing and exploding everywhere. A fragment from one of these shells, or a ball from a case shot, struck Christopher Erickson in the chest. It was very likely a mortal wound, but hell was not finished with the young lieutenant yet. The tough Norwegian rode toward the rear, toward the hypothetical main Union line back on Cemetery Ridge.

Meanwhile, the Federal artillery along Wheatfield Road began to withdraw. McGilvery told his battery commanders to get their guns away before so many of their horses were shot that the pieces could not be moved. One by one along the line they hitched up their cannons and limbers as shells screamed toward them from three directions. The undulating field behind Bigelow's battery streamed with hurrying teams and crews. Bigelow's men tensely waited for their turn, but when it came Kershaw's South Carolinians were so close that Bigelow couldn't bring his horses forward: the Confederates would have shot them down while the crews were hitching up the guns. So he ordered one of the oddest maneuvers ever necessitated during the Civil War: "Retire by prolonge, firing." A prolonge is the heavy rope wound at the bottom of a cannon's trail. The crews unspooled each gun's rope and either pulled it themselves or tied it to a team. Not being hitched to their limbers, the guns could still be fired. This firing kept the Rebels cautious because the field dips and rolls and you cannot see what is beyond the next ripple. The recoils rolled the pieces back, assisting Bigelow's men and horses.

At a fence corner at the bottom of the field, four hundred yards from his Wheatfield Road position, Bigelow prepared to order the first piece through the gate. His battery had barely made it, and in fact they were not clear yet. While the field they were leaving sloped upward back toward the peach orchard, concealing the retreating battery, it also concealed the Rebels. Each discharge made the Southerners hesitate to come over the crest, but soon enough they would come on with a rush from two, possibly three, sides. Already some of Kershaw's men were filtering through the woods along the sloping field, intending to cut off the 9th's retreat. Bigelow looked past the fence corner toward the other batteries strung out toward Cemetery Ridge.

At that moment, his commander, Lieutenant Colonel McGilvery, rode up and told Bigelow to halt and turn his battery. "The crisis of the engagement had now arrived," McGilvery wrote in his battle report.[3] There was no infantry in position on lower Cemetery Ridge. McGilvery needed time to assemble batteries to hold back the Confederate offensive while General Hancock brought over some units from his 2d Corps. The 9th Massachusetts Battery would have to stay here and buy him that time. It would be expensive.

Captain Bigelow sized up the corner of the field and decided that there was room to work only four of his six guns. He motioned for one of his sections to go on through and save itself, but a piece overturned at the gate, blocking the way. The other crew whipped their team up over the low stone fence — a maneuver theoretically impossible, evincing the motivational power of the Rebel Yell at close quarters.

Kershaw's men were coming through the woods to the left and rear, over the top of the hill, and now the 21st Mississippi of Barksdale's brigade showed up to the right front. In minutes they would work their way around the right to the battery's rear. As the remaining four guns went into action, Christopher Erickson rode up. Nobody knows why. Nobody knows whether he had looked for medical help and could not find any, whether he suddenly felt well, whether he got angry, or whether he knew he was dying and might as well have one more swing of the battle axe at the enemy. But there is no doubt about what happened to the young Norwegian in the next few minutes.

A good while ago someone wrote a book called *The Man Nobody Knows*. That book, about the founder of Christianity, became a bestseller and stayed around for years. When in 1958 Richard N. Current published a book about little known and little understood facets of Abraham Lincoln, he titled it *The Lincoln Nobody Knows*. Openly paying Current the handsome compliment of theft, Gabor S. Boritt gathered essays on little known or controversial aspects of the famous battle and christened the result *The Gettysburg Nobody Knows*.[4] This essay extends the compliment by being titled "The Gettysburg Nobody Knows"—a more direct larceny, but certainly a petty one. However, the present naming is the most accurate. What we got before was actually The Man Somebody Thinks He Knows, The Lincoln Somebody Knows, and The Gettysburg a Few of Us Know—And Soon Quite a Few More Will Know. But we are concerned here quite literally with the Gettysburg nobody knows.

With some accuracy we can plot the movements of the 9th Massachusetts Battery across the field. (We will never know exactly at what time.) We know that Bigelow's crews fired three tons of ammunition, including ninety-two rounds of canister. Perhaps sixty or so of those rounds were fired by four of Bigelow's crews from the Trostle Farm fence corner as they were attacked by Kershaw's men and by the 21st Mississippi. But we do not know how Bigelow's gunners felt as they sponged the brass Napoleons while bullets hissed around them, clanged off the tubes, or chunked into limbers, horses, and men; we do not know how black powder smoke feels in lungs quickened by the sight of enemy infantry emerging in line of battle over a rise a hundred yards away; nor can we feel the "peculiar corkscrew sensation" the Rebel Yell sent up the spine as one saw red flags hazily coming through the smoke. We know what some of the soldiers at Gettysburg did, but we do not know what they experienced.

We do not know the fight the soldiers knew, nor do we know

exactly what happened almost anywhere on the field. We do not know why some significant things came about. Why was Col. Strong Vincent passing by with his brigade exactly when a staff officer went riding to find troops to defend Little Round Top, and why was the Iron Brigade's 6th Wisconsin regiment held in reserve on the morning of July 1 and therefore able to charge the Railroad Cut, or why did Bigelow's battery draw last place in line on the Wheatfield Road, or why couldn't Stonewall Jackson have been alive on the evening of the first day's fighting?

There are "black holes" in the historian's Gettysburg—a phrase used by William Frassanito to describe the absence of information concerning a part of the battle at the Rose Farm, down the slope in front of the 9th Massachusetts Battery's original position.[5] There are no written accounts of the 10th, 15th, and 53d Georgia of Brig. Gen. Paul Semmes's Brigade, or of Kershaw's 15th South Carolina, in the battle on that part of the field. Yet we know they fought there: we have photographs of their dead. Evidence was palpable, yet exactly how the evidence arrived remains unknown. It need not always remain unknown, however. The ravenous activities of today's Civil War scholarship may yet turn up letters in an attic, or a journal deep in an old chest, or a report that somehow got filed in the wrong place.

It used to be little known that decisive actions took place near the Lutheran seminary on day one. It remains a surprise to many people that a few Southern women fought at Gettysburg, their bodies, clad in Confederate uniforms, discovered by burial parties after the battle. It may never be known for sure how many men Lee really lost in Pennsylvania—more than were reported, certainly, possibly by the thousands. This is only the beginning of a list of what we don't know. There are things people did not know before; there are things lacking documentation today; there are controversial issues. But all these mysteries may be solved someday. What we are concerned with here is what we *cannot know*—not because facts are missing, but because of the nature of knowledge, and because of our own nature. These things are actually more important than facts, and simply to know what *kinds of things they are* moves us from mere knowledge toward understanding.

Knowledge can be valuable in itself, but that value is limited. With the facts, we can be entertained, informed in a small way, even have a certain kind of power, though a poor power. Someone can always surprise or impress us with a new bit of knowledge. What we want, however, is wisdom—*human* knowledge; and we want understanding—knowledge of things beyond our human boundaries. Why do things happen as they do? Why are we here? What are we to do? Where do good and evil come from? After we die, shall we live again? It is the knowledge we cannot have that most requires answers, and most rewards seeking.

When Lieutenant Erickson returned to the embattled 9th Massachusetts Battery, he said he was thirsty. A man handed up a canteen which — it not being vinegar on a sponge — Erickson drained in one long draft. He then proceeded to direct his two guns as the Rebels came on, yipping, firing, flattening to the ground, and rushing up a few yards while the gun facing them was being reloaded.

Before long, men in gray and butternut were swarming all around the battery, though keeping some distance. They did not have to brave the guns' blasts in one frontal rush. They could afford to be a little patient — or so they thought. Some South Carolinians slipped from tree to tree, firing as they went, eventually getting to the fence behind the left section. Mississippians moved around the farm buildings across the little road at the fence corner. While the guns were being served — as the crews rushed through their discipline of loading, ramming, and sighting the pieces, then shoving in double and triple loads of canister, thumbing the touch holes, pulling the lanyards, and heaving the guns back into place, concentrating on the hot work at hand, beclouded by smoke in that low corner of the field and deaf to single rifle shots — Mississippians coolly took aim at the Yankees working to mow down their comrades. Some of the Southerners loped around directly behind the battery and climbed up on the parked caissons. They stood and aimed, carefully killing the cannoneers while a ragged but heavy line in front closed in, firing steadily. "It was a wonder anyone survived," one of the Massachusetts men wrote afterward.

Lieutenant Erickson was looking down on his two crews, perhaps shouting an order, when five Confederates, all very close, each took careful aim at the mounted officer and fired pretty much together. Struck five times, Erickson fell dead from the saddle. He had come a long way, across an ocean — not to mention having lived across the span of more than twenty-five years — to have it ended in this rural fence corner. To have what ended?

The fight at the Trostle Farm did not pause for Lieutenant Erickson's death, but History offers an opportunity for us to linger. What he had no chance to ask, we can ask; indeed we must ask, because no man is an island, entire of himself. What absurdity or necessity brought

Christopher Erickson from the beautiful country of his birth to this little hell in front of Cemetery Ridge? What is the nature of the life he voluntarily held forward within reach of chaos and death? What have we seen, and what has escaped us?

We do not know why Lieutenant Erickson was seated on his horse behind his section of guns as Kershaw's men surrounded it. We do know that he enlisted on July 31, 1862, at the age of twenty-seven, and that he had been a cabinetmaker living in Boston. He must have had military experience in Europe, because he went in as a first lieutenant. He was commissioned into the 9th Massachusetts Light Artillery on October 8,[6] but we do not know why this immigrant enlisted, what feelings or convictions impelled him, or why he enlisted on the day he did rather than on another and so eventually became part of the 9th Massachusetts Battery instead of some other unit. We do not know how it happened that a certain Confederate gunner aimed his shot just so, and the fuse was trimmed just that length — not a quarter-second shorter or longer, the matter of a tenth of a centimeter perhaps — or why the metal of the shell came apart exactly along the lines it did, sending one jagged patch of iron on that precise line into Erickson's chest.

> What immortal hand or eye
> Dare frame that fearful symmetry?

Nor do we know what moved five Southerners to fire at the mounted man, or why these same men or others did not shoot and kill Captain Bigelow also. In short, we know everything about 1st Lt. Christopher Erickson except *that which mattered most to him;* and except that which gave his life and death personal meaning. If we are not objects, then neither were those men at Gettysburg. We are not ready to consider History to be a science, impersonal by definition. On the personal level, Christopher Erickson is related to us. Why was he there and why did it happen to him and for what? We do not know anything about *why,* or *how,* or *what if.* As the French writer Saint-Exupery wrote, "What is essential is invisible to the eye."[7]

One morning, Robert Frost observed the freakish coincidence of an albino spider perched on a miscolored white heal-all (normally a blue flower). The white combination had lured a moth through the night. Looking at the stiff, dead moth, Frost asks the terrible question:

> What had that flower to do with being white,
> The wayside blue and innocent heal-all?

What brought the kindred spider to that height,
Then steered the white moth thither in the night?
What but design of darkness to appall? —
If design govern in a thing so small.[8]

Even the great Battle of Gettysburg was pretty small, when we lift our gaze a little. If you go out West and look up at the night sky, glittering in its fathomless deep with stars upon stars sprinkled, gathered, in the dense, incandescent streak we call the Milky Way — if we consider that there are more *galaxies* in the universe than there are stars in that Milky Way — then we wonder "if design govern in a thing so small" as humanity.

> When I consider thy heavens, the work of thy fingers, the moon and the stars, which thou hast ordained; what is man, that thou art mindful of him? and the son of man, that thou visitest him?

An answer is in the Gettysburg nobody knows.

The young Norwegian and his men had bought enough time for McGilvery to build his row of artillery, and the great attack by Longstreet's and Hill's corps began to wear itself out against the Cemetery Ridge line. But we are still left wondering why. Plenty of South Carolinians and Mississippians facing Bigelow's guns died too, buying nothing except shallow graves in Pennsylvania soil. The universe is unforgiving. We live under the conditions of tragedy. Everything has consequences, but we do not know much about what consequences will follow from our actions. We do not even know what is going into the decisions we make. Everything that matters comes from beyond our knowledge or control. In the words of The Man Nobody Knows, "The wind bloweth where it listeth, and thou hearest the sound thereof, but canst not tell whence it cometh, and whither it goeth."[9] Why did Erickson buy a ticket on that specific ship in Norway? It cost him his life. Never mind why he joined the Union army: he was a dead man the minute he heard about America.

It is our fate to make tragic mistakes. The universe operates by law and it has no mercy. We do not know what those laws are, yet their effects on us are most intimately personal. If there are such things as mercy or justice, hope or purpose, they must come from something, somewhere, or someone greater than the universe itself. Whether something or someone greater than the universe exists seems to be for us to decide, but in any case the mystery involved is our only chance for a break.

Visitors to Gettysburg today sometimes feel a mysterious presence, so it seems to have outlasted one Gettysburg nobody knows: the real battle as it happened back in 1863. The mystery seems to be more enduring than fate, freedom, or chance. We do not understand the sacrament of our own blood. That is, we know its elements but not its meaning; nor do we know whether believing in its significance is an act of faith or delusion.

Lieutenant Erickson did not know the thousands of lives he ruled out by the one life he chose. Every yes means a thousand noes, and vice versa. Just as what would have happened had Dan Sickles not gone forward is a Gettysburg nobody knows, so are all the things we have decided against the lives that nobody knows.

These unknowns, like the apparently unused space in Japanese paintings, give shape and substance to what we know. The dead at Gettysburg number in the millions, and their sacrifices make us what we are. Photographs of the dead show men whose lives we do not understand, with countless invisible multitudes behind them — the very atmosphere of what is. Over that field, even before the work of flies, buzzards, and burial details began, the work of time proceeded, and still continues, exponentially multiplying the unknowns.

Lieutenant Christopher Erickson offered his life as a personal gift to us. A most significant unknown is what we will do with that gift.

Here is a familiar quotation from Ezekiel 37:

> The hand of the LORD was upon me, and carried me out . . . and set me down into the midst of the valley which was full of bones . . . and, lo, they were very dry. And he said unto me, Son of man . . . Prophecy upon these bones, and say unto them, O ye dry bones . . . I will cause breath to enter into you, and ye shall live. . . . I prophesied . . . and as I prophesied, there was a noise, and behold a shaking, and the bones came together, bone to bone. And when I beheld, lo, the sinews and the flesh came up upon them, and the skin covered them above: but there was no breath in them.[10]

We resemble the prophet Ezekiel at that point. What we discover as researchers can fit bone to bone and fact to fact. But lo, we cannot put breath into those slain. We cannot bring those spirits, or the invisible forces that moved them, back to those minutes of crisis on July 2, 1863. They gave our particular lives to us. Their lives run in a current to ours, person to person.

Historians might not want to be philosophers and poets also, but we readers must be all these together and more, because we have everything at stake. We must live in this world; we must choose and act. The very least to be said for sure about the value of unknowns is that they keep the boundaries open. We must seek in order to find. Understanding how little we know is the beginning of wisdom.

They teach the elements really of ignorance, not of knowledge.
— THOREAU

Somebody's Darling

About the fifth time I watched the movie *Gettysburg*, there was a college student in the room, a visitor from a sophisticated and prestigious Eastern college. She was not a History major; she did not even know exactly what year Gettysburg had been fought or how many days it had taken to fight it. But she sat on the end of the couch and settled down with the rest of us to watch at least the first half of that celluloid tome.

I had made up my mind beforehand not to say anything during the movie, but only to answer whatever questions anybody might have then or later. From the opening scene, as fluid lines of march seep upward across the map of Virginia, "Mary-Land," and Pennsylvania — until near the end of Part One, when I finally realized something had gone way wrong with this young lady — I tried to remember what had made this error-riddled film so powerful the first time I saw it.

One of the worst things about the movie *Gettysburg* is that there is no satisfactory sense of Robert E. Lee. It worries me that future generations might be influenced by the inadequate and misleading portrayal of this man who became an epic hero of our epic war. A friend gave me a calendar with Gettysburg scenes painted by one of the most popular Civil War painters. I did not know whether to laugh or to snarl when I flipped a page and discovered that the General Lee in the calendar was the face of Martin Sheen. In fact, all the major figures portrayed on the calendar were represented by the actors who had played them in the movie *Gettysburg*. If you stop at the Cashtown Inn on the old Chambersburg Pike near Gettysburg, where Robert E. Lee and James Longstreet and A. P. Hill rode past on July 1, 1863, you will find numerous portraits on the dining room walls. Many of them are not of Civil War soldiers but of actors who played them in *Gettysburg*. Instead of Robert E. Lee and John Buford, you get Martin Sheen and Sam Elliott. I would rather that future Civil War students see the few black and white still photographs of Gen. Robert E. Lee than the full-color, walking, talking, dreaming Martin Sheen dressed up for the movie.

Of course Martin Sheen does a great job in the movie; in fact you are thinking throughout the whole movie what a great job Martin Sheen is doing — which means of course that the game is up. It's like the old line about a monkey riding a bicycle: the point is not how well the thing is done, but that the thing is done at all. Robert E. Lee was a tall soldier whose very presence awed every man and whose looks struck every woman. So, considering that Mr. Sheen is a short man with a paunch, he does a job worthy of the excellent actor he is. But it isn't Robert E. Lee. Nor does Sheen speak with the right Virginia accent — or so I have been told by a Southern Civil War scholar familiar with tidewater accents. I think it's worse that the character says "very" too much, however peculiarly it is pronounced. But these complaints are trivial.

The real problem is in the script, which comes from Michael Shaara's excellent novel, *The Killer Angels*.[1] Regardless of that book's many wonders, it does a bad job of imagining General Lee. I do not mean simply that Shaara adopted the revisionist viewpoint of, for example, Glenn Tucker's *Lee and Longstreet at Gettysburg* — one of the studies that finally exonerated General Longstreet from unjust blame for the Confederate loss of the battle, and placed ultimate responsibility for major decisions and mistakes with General Lee.[2] The real problem in Shaara's novel and in the movie *Gettysburg* is that by overdrawing on the Longstreet account, the writers make Lee something other than what he was.

One has to explain why Lee ordered Pickett's Charge. That blunder has been a great obstacle and stumbling block to anyone trying to understand or justify one of history's great commanders. Admirers and analysts of Robert E. Lee are obligated to come to grips with such gross errors as Pickett's Charge and Malvern Hill on their way to describing a general whose brilliance, audacity, character, thoroughness, and leadership saved a Confederacy that was circling the drain in May of 1862, preserved its life two or three years beyond its time, and almost thwarted Ulysses S. Grant's all-fronts onslaught in 1864.

Shaara explains Pickett's Charge, but fails to explain the rest; and that casts doubt on his explanation of Pickett's Charge. That is, we get in Shaara and the movie a somewhat infirm general who in a gentle and dignified manner is touched in the head. The character is an enthusiast — what Mark Twain would have called a "miraculous fool." It is certainly quite possible that the fortuitous but only apparent "victory" of the first day's battle struck Lee as providential — that is, providential in the South's favor — and that it was God's will that the Yankees crumble. But if the Yankees were going to crumble, it was in part because they were Yankees. Lee believed his boys could always move them in a face-to-face fight.

In other words, Lee's religion was not a pious enthusiasm that stood by itself. Lee liked the psalm that blesses the Lord, "who teaches my fingers to fight."[3] God might ordain victory, but Lee and his men would have to fight for it. This fighter is missing from *The Killer Angels* and the movie *Gettysburg*. So is the Lee who underestimated Yankees.

It is doubtful that anybody thoroughly understands Robert E. Lee. Emory Thomas's recent biography of Lee lays out a factual and balanced picture, but in a somewhat satisfied manner that lacks the tension and uncertainty one should feel in the presence of this awe-inspiring, flawed, and grand figure. In biography, nobody ever really has control of their material.[4] Perhaps the worshipful, unfair, oversimplified masterpiece of Douglas Southall Freeman has come closest to Lee because the grandeur one must always face in dealing with General Lee is present in force — albeit at the expense of reasonable accounts of his failures and weaknesses. Perhaps if you jammed Alan Nolan's *Lee Considered* and Freeman's *R. E. Lee* together, threw in Lee's wartime papers and all his letters, added some Virginia soil and a few books of the King James Bible, and then stirred in an unspecified quantity of flesh and blood, you might get material to shape a rough-hewn bust of the man. But the essential *expression* of the general and college president, and the invisible soul — these would remain a fascinating and mysterious blank.[5] Lee's character must be portrayed widely: when you have one characteristic or one action fully explained, you probably have not explained anything at all. I would not want to face Robert E. Lee in battle, but I would be glad to play ping-pong against the dreamy chump in the movie *Gettysburg*.

In watching the film again I was reminded that each time I see it, new irritants emerge every few minutes. They overwhelm my initial engrossment in the movie, and I seem to have forgotten why I ever thought it was good.

Even the first time I very much regretted the use of reenactors in the film. It was a great experience for them, they report, and we are assured of authentic uniforms in *Gettysburg*—and most of all, the movie would not have been made without them, because they came cheaply, like the originals, out of devotion to the cause. But they're a bunch of forty- and fifty-year-old men, culled from the desks and 'burbs of today's America—without the benefit of two years' marching the dusty roads of rural nineteenth-century America, without two winters of camp and drill, and without seven hundred days of bad food, hunger, loneliness, boredom, terror, killing, and dysentery.

Early in the movie the scout Harrison is challenged by a Confederate picket line commanded by a white-haired, seventy-year-old man who almost could have doubled for Burl Ives. How did this guy get up here from Virginia? Motorcycle? After Pickett's Charge the idiot camera dwells on a huge hill of a man, at least four hundred pounds, limping back from Cemetery Hill with some kind of makeshift crutch. What happened to the "lean and hungry set of wolves" an observer described when "Lee's Miserables" crossed the Potomac the year before? If you don't like to watch basketball because ten millionaires playing ball is distasteful to you, you won't want to watch *Gettysburg* because it is a thousand baby boomers playing war.

But the first time I saw the movie, it worked—although I could not now remember why.

After Harrison is brought in by Burl Ives, he confronts General Longstreet at the corps commander's tent. The character does not take the risks that Sheen's Lee does, and so does not fall into so many obvious errors. But this "Longstreet" errs in the opposite direction: less is certainly less. With *Gettysburg's* Longstreet, throw away the beard and the hat, and there ain't much left. Except the word *sir*.

If Ron Maxwell had been administered an electric shock every time he put the word "Sir?" into the script, we might have had some real talk. As it is, the dialogue is very, very weak. It is apparent in weak performances, such as Tom Chamberlain's report to his brother about how terrible, terrible things were with the wounded and dying, but it also cuts off strong performances at the knees.

Jeff Daniels, of course, does a terrific job playing Col. Joshua Lawrence Chamberlain of the 20th Maine. The apex of the performance — as perhaps during the actual 20th's Gettysburg campaign — is Chamberlain's speech to the mutinous men of the 2d Maine, who have been put under the 20th Maine's guard but who insist they will not fight. Getting these men to fight was one of Chamberlain's greatest services, for without them his Maine regiment would have been overrun on Little Round Top despite the advantages of position and physical well-being. The colonel's presence and manner, so well-imagined by Daniels, must have inspired the reluctant men of the 2d Maine as much as what he said. What he says in the movie is pretty good, too — until at the end he says that what we are really fighting for here, men, is "each other." That's great stuff for a bunch of aging reenactors in 1990, but I do not suppose it would have made a lot of sense to the twenty-year-olds who in 1863 were fighting to protect the Union, their homes and families, wives and children, and perhaps to abolish slavery — and had not gone to college or attended sensitivity training sessions in the 1960s and '70s. In battle, soldiers fight for each other, but the inspirational speech is a different matter. Likewise after Pickett's Charge, when Tom and Lawrence Chamberlain hugged, silhouetted by the sunset, I was afraid they were going to smooch.

Nevertheless I too was moved at the end of the film, though it is hard to remember why. The Civil War era was sentimental, even lachrymose, in ways I do not think the 1970s effectively translated. It is hard to imagine Brigadier General Buford, otherwise superbly played by Sam Elliott, brushing a tear from his eye when Maj. Gen. John Reynolds and his splendid 1st Corps infantry come to the relief of his cavalry.

That minute, up in the cupola of the Lutheran seminary, is one of my favorites in the movie — especially the shot superimposed upon the 1860s photograph — colored in — of the town from Seminary Ridge. It is ingenious and delightful, despite the fact that the photo shows the aftermath of the fight that is just beginning.

The cinematic action of Buford's cavalry holding back Bubba Heth's Confederate infantry leaves some factuality to be desired. We see them battling it out from behind a fence rail barricade as the Rebels come to within ten or twenty yards and Buford says with clenched teeth, "Hold that flank. Hold it!" In fact, no such knockdown, drag-out fight took place until the Federal infantry arrived. But people who have not studied the battle, like the girl sitting at the end of the couch, cannot be expected to know that.

A little later in the movie we hear three Confederates from Brig. Gen. James Archer's brigade say they were captured in the Railroad Cut. Now, people have heard of Archer's Tennesseans, and people have heard of the Railroad Cut, but this movie is the first time anyone has ever heard of them both together. It is so annoying to see error after error come before your eyes in a movie touted by its makers for its authenticity, that you wonder why you are watching it again.

In that early segment of the movie, when "Longstreet" takes off his sombrero and goes into Lee's tent to talk about Harrison's report on Yankee movements, you have another entertaining but improbable scene. (I am told that they had to shoot it several times because the actors themselves were so entertained by Lee's line, "We move on the word of an actor?") The script cannot resist stooping to melodrama in this scene. The generals are bending over a map. Longstreet and Lee both observe that several roads converge at a town between them and the fast-marching Union army. But Lee has been looking at the map without his spectacles! He tells Longstreet that he left the glasses over there, pointing behind him—the tent is not large—so he cannot read the name of the town, and Longstreet gets to deadpan for us, "Gettysburg." That he pronounces it incorrectly, for a man who has probably heard the name from a scout and at any rate is a Southerner, is not a great injury to the movie. We ought not get exercised by the word of an actor.

The generals in the movie, like the generals in *The Killer Angels*, certainly belong to the leisure class. Otherwise they could not supply the lengths of meaningful dialogue we get after hours, when the armies knock off, kick back, and do campfires. Otherwise, the generals would be acting like there was a war on: harried, distracted, short of sleep, trying to patch up their commands, procure supplies and ammunition, analyze casualty reports and replace officers, figure out what had happened to them that day and what would happen the next, and get their men rested enough to be up and ready at four A.M.

One of these campfire scenes brings about the greatest howler of the movie. The generals who will make Pickett's Charge the next day are talking about the theory of evolution. It might be that you and I are descended from "a ape," says Stephen Lang, who creates a wonderful Pickett character, but do not try to tell me that General Lee is descended from "a ape." That closes the discussion on apes, monkeys, Darwin, and evolution. Then we go to "Longstreet's" tent and a close-up of the general (Tom Berenger) in half-light, with his Wal-Mart beard all around his face, and he looks like a — guess what? A ape.

I do not really think that effect was intended, and I hate to mention it.* Different people see different things. The unprepared eye would not see Brigadier General Buford riding in front of a row of his own guns while they are firing. Some people would not see the same images used twice during the artillery bombardment. Some would object that the adulation of Lee happened during the war but not at Gettysburg. (The reenactors somehow felt so convinced by Martin Sheen that they saw someone nobody else had seen for over a hundred years.) I wonder why somebody did not see that Jeb Stuart looked all wrong: The great, exuberant, but unspeakably chagrined cavalry commander was portrayed by a thin fellow somebody forced into clothing and a beard too big for him. It is hard to see the 20th Maine's "Sergeant Kilrain" as a veteran, a seasoned soldier who has marched thousands of miles — where? In what wars, what campaigns? When he's wounded on Little Round Top, Kilrain's attempt to raise and fire his musket ranks with the best efforts of little boys playing battle. Fortunately, someone who had just got ready to fire must have been knocked out of action, so theoretically we are spared the absurdity of the one-armed sergeant loading a musket using leverage and grimaces. Still, people see something in Kilrain that makes them believe in him. Battlefield guides will tell you that people ask to see the spot of ground where he was wounded. I tried to ignore the Kilrain images as I watched the 20th Maine's battle on Little Round Top.

From the standpoint of accuracy, perhaps the worst thing about the movie is that there is no realistic gore to show graphically what really happened. No detached arms cartwheel into the air, no bullets burst through bodies, no faces crack in blood. As the 15th Alabama came on yet again, it occurred to me that what the movie lacks in realism, it makes up for in error.

But it also should have occurred to me that there is no such thing as complete accuracy, in "History" or in historical fiction. It is all a representation, more or less informed but never a copy of what happened, and what counts is whether the symbols we choose — words or characters — convey something false or something essential. Saint-Exupery wrote, "It is only with the heart that one can see rightly."[6]

I had become so engrossed in the 20th Maine's fight — firing its

---

*But my friend Paul R. Landefeld Jr. informs me that the scientific name for the mountain gorilla is *Gorilla gorilla berengi*. One bows to inevitability.

volleys in the woods on Little Round Top, blasting into the very faces of the 15th Alabama clambering up the hill, men yelling, screaming, groaning, spinning when struck, jolting backward as men shot them, reforming and coming on again, bracing to receive another charge — I had been so absorbed that it must have taken me a couple of minutes to realize that the couch was trembling, shaking a little. I looked over at the student sitting on the end. She said later that what she saw was men being killed. She saw the essential. She remembered to do what we have forgotten how to do — we scholars, we buffs, we historians, we experts, we critics. She cried.

Ghosts of Gettysburg

A few years ago, one of the Civil War magazines ran an article on a land exchange deal done in Gettysburg. The writer condemned the deal because it gave one of Gettysburg's private enterprises a part of the battlefield the owners wanted in exchange for a piece of the Gettysburg National Military Park. According to the author, who happens to be an acquaintance of mine, the Park Service was a sucker, trading off valuable acres for land of relatively little interest. The new owners, presumably to preempt buyer's remorse or any notion of undoing the deal, totally bulldozed their acquired acres on New Year's Day, when nobody was looking, thereby erasing a historic place forever. They then commenced construction of a sports facility. My acquaintance closed his article pointedly, with nice rhetorical balance, if somewhat histrionically: "Where brave men died, now rich boys play."

The author is an interesting and in some ways heroic man himself. He quit his job back in 1977 in order to do Civil War stuff full-time. I don't mean he *retired*. He was a young man then, hoping to make a living by writing about the war. For twenty years, during which most of us would have left the field and gone back in pusillanimous defeat to our desks and offices and Rolodexes and Volvos, this man scribbled, scribbled, scribbled—like Edward Gibbon, but without much financial reward. Indeed, he barely scraped by, jobbing out for all kinds of short-term gigs while remaining faithful to his inclination and his calling.

Then he sold a pamphlet titled *Ghosts of Gettysburg* to a local publisher. There was no distribution of that booklet outside Gettysburg; it was hawked around to drugstores and put on racks next to chewing gum, postcards, and *True Romances*. But tourists bought that thing like there was no tomorrow. (I was one of them.) Now there are *More Ghosts of Gettysburg*, and *Ghosts of Gettysburg III*, and I would not be surprised if the next time I visit the town I see *Son of Ghosts of Gettysburg* or *Return of Ghosts of Gettysburg*. He might well be branching out to Antietam and who knows where else. There are *Ghosts of Gettysburg* videos on sale now, and if you walk the streets of Gettysburg on almost any evening of the year you might see one of my acquaintance's spinoffs dressed in a hoopskirt or high collar and 1860s cravat, swinging an antique lantern while walking down the sidewalk with a gaggle of tourists in tow: there are now Ghosts of Gettysburg Tours. The *Ghosts* author does not drive a Mercedes, but the man is not poor anymore.

Here are some examples from *Ghosts III*. A woman was driving a pickup back to a reenactors' campsite during the filming of the movie *Gettysburg*. At night.

> She looked in the rear-view mirror. The mirror gave her something more than just a look back from where she had come; it suddenly was looking back in time, for there, in the formerly empty bed of the truck, were several Civil War–era soldiers. They sat, half a dozen historical anachronisms, weary and tattered, riding from the town where the woman had just dropped off their imitators, back out into the darkened fields of sacrifice more familiar to them than the neon-lighted modern town of Gettysburg. They said not a word, but just stared with that strange look in their eyes — the "thousand-yard stare," they would call it in a later war — or as one poet put it, with the sad eyes of a newborn beast of burden.[1]

When she got to the camp's checkpoint, she rolled down her window and tremulously asked the guard whether he saw anybody in the back of her truck. Guess whether he did or didn't.

Then there are the two ladies out for a stroll one evening. They pass an old house on Steinwehr Avenue and happen to look in a window. They see what they think are wax figures: one was a woman "dressed all in black" sitting in a rocking chair, and

> right in front of her . . . was a cot. Lying on the cot was a man, dressed in something dark. The woman looked like she was in mourning. The man seemed . . . dead.

The house was a commercial establishment, and the next day during business hours the ladies came back and went in. They walked around, bewildered, and finally asked, "Where are the wax figures?"

There were no wax figures. It was a craft shop. Furthermore, the cot had been alongside a wall near a door, and neither the wall nor the door were to be seen. Wait a minute. There was a pegboard holding craft items back there — and behind it a wall and door that had been covered several months previously. That house was the place where the body of Maj. Gen. John Reynolds had been carried on the morning of July 1, and where it lay while the general's aides all left to try to find a coffin. That section in the book is titled, "Tourist Season in the Other World."[2]

There are quite a few good ones in these booklets: the boy whose face appears at an upper-story dormitory window, the sentry who stands atop a Gettysburg College building, a soldier who cannot seem to get out of an old basement on the seminary grounds, and this one:

> She was standing in the newer section of the house during a quiet time of day. Suddenly she had a feeling that someone was watching her. She turned and looked toward the original front door of the old part of the house — the door on the south side of the structure — and there to her amazement stood a soldier dressed in a "cream-colored, butternut uniform," with long reddish or auburn hair and a scraggly beard and moustache. She described him as wearing a floppy, sweat-stained, butternut-colored hat. She saw he had a blanket roll on his back, attached across his chest with what she thought were canvas straps. He was very skinny and gaunt and very pale. She saw that he carried a long rifle, "almost as tall as he was," which seemed to her to be a good six feet. They stood and gazed directly into each other's eyes.
>
> She recalled that it seemed he stood there for minutes, his direct gaze piercing hers, although upon reflection, she figured it may have been only 15 or 20 seconds. As he looked directly at her she said he wore an expression of extreme sadness in his eyes — so sad, in fact, that she actually felt his sadness. "It looked," she said "as if he'd really been through hell. He just looked at me as if to say, 'please help me,' or 'please feel sorry for me.'" She said she didn't feel threatened, just sad. Suddenly he was gone, dematerializing before her eyes.[3]

The chapter is titled "Alone in Hell."

Now, the easy thing to conclude would be that these intriguing, entertaining, even frightening stories that make use of the brave men who struggled and died in a battle are worse than a land deal that obliterated a section of a railroad cut that men fought and died to defend and capture. The land deal might have been pure greed, but these ghost stories are very impure greed: they exploit dead husbands and fathers who gave the last full measure of devotion for the noblest ideals ever to appear in this materialistic country. But to accuse the author, Mark Nesbitt, of being an exploiter would be, as I said, too easy — besides being hypocritical, self-righteous, and ironic. It is not so simple.

First, Mr. Nesbitt can be a serious Civil War writer who deserves some success. He has written a book about Jeb Stuart, for example, examining and defending the behavior of Lee's cavalier cavalry leader during the Gettysburg campaign. One does not have to agree with any of the conclusions to realize that the author, like his subject, took great chances back in 1977, risking total failure in order to achieve success. The Civil War's great generals did that. It was generals like McClellan, on the other hand, who feared to fail and hesitated to employ all of their resources. Most of us are like McClellan, and we admire or are jealous of the Jeb Stuarts in life. What I am saying here could easily become an exercise in envy.

More important, Maj. Gen. John F. Reynolds and that pale young man in butternut both died so that we could be entrepreneurs. Every time we exert our labor in this free market and receive material benefits from it, we are using the blood of our Civil War forebears, building our enterprises on their graves. These honored dead gave their lives so that we could do exactly what Ford Motor Company wants us to do: make money and spend it. Didn't they?

Freedom, you might say, is more than economic opportunity, and liberty more than lucre; justice is more important to produce than is the Gross National Product. That last one always comes along to spoil things. Justice. Perhaps more important than the economic *use* made of justice is the principle of justice itself: that each person has value, equal to all others, and that value stands qualitatively beyond and above economic value.

Well then, two things become apparent. The first is that we need to ask whether *Ghosts of Gettysburg* or any art, history, writing, or commercial enterprise does justice to the men who died in the Civil War, and does justice to the people who see, read, and consume today — those of us longing to find the truth and, like the perennial masses, yearning to be free.

But before we judge Mark Nesbitt one way or the other by that criterion, let us leave it behind, judging not, that we ourselves be not judged, as Lincoln reminds us — because the second point emerges larger, its immediacy overwhelming the first issue and relegating it to the category of historical curiosities. The immediate issue is whether or not we do justice to ourselves and to our fellow man and woman. For if we do not, we trample upon the graves of martyrs and mock the blood they shed worse than if we had bought and sold the land for which they fought. Unless we do justice to each other, we have sold the very ideal for which they died.

The last story in *Ghosts III* tells about an inn that stood west of town. It was used for a hospital, filled with dying and bleeding men. Afterward it became a plain old inn again for years and years, and everyone was content, copacetic, and prosperous — *until*, as the author phrases it, "Hell made a house call."[4]

It is the petty practice of reviewers and critics and carpers to pick out a writer's cheesiest phrase and burp it back up in print — but in this case that melodramatic phrase about hell is quite appropriate. It reminds one of the soldier who wrote home, "we have gettin nuthin but hell & lots uv it."[5]

A ghost story, thrilling as it might be, is not nearly as frightening as war. The rappings of a ghost are not as terrible as the reproach of the dead. And the things we do to each other are more terrifying than the ghosts of anywhere. Whatever we do, we do to ourselves ultimately, and the final fright would be to have bought and sold and added field to field until, to use Nesbitt's words again, we are "Alone in Hell."

There is a chasm between knowledge and ignorance
which the arches of science can never span.
— THOREAU

A Ghost Story

Late last night I heard sharp knocking at my son's closed bedroom door. I awakened fully, clearly, though I had been sleeping soundly. Two quick raps I heard distinctly — told myself he'd gotten up. But no further sound came after; I sat breathless and intent. Maybe he was ill or frightened, had a dream or couldn't sleep. Maybe it had been my door.

It was now bleak mid-December. Clear, cold moonlight through my window wrought long ghosts on the floor. Timers had shut off my light and cut the furnace hours ago. An open book lay in my lap, a pale companion. Stiff and cold, I hurried to my chamber door. Quietly I turned the doorknob and looked out into the hall. Darkness there and nothing more.

The book I have been reading, reading — for it is a long, long book — is the more-or-less forgotten volume *Independent People*, out of print for thirty years. But its author, Halldor Laxness, won the Nobel Prize for it in 1955. It is a great book, this early-twentieth-century Icelandic epic, or mock epic: it affects you, creeps over you, makes you laugh and almost weep, until you come to believe every word of it. In fact, the book probably explains the rapping I heard.

Independent People dawns when Iceland is first settled, A.D. 894, and we read of a curse put upon the valley our modern "hero," or antihero, will farm. Gunnvor, a woman executed and dismembered for grisly things she did with the help of an evil spirit, still haunts a remote valley in northern Iceland—a valley "where the centuries lie side by side."[1] She perpetrated "the great spectral visitations" of 1750 and is still present—so much feared that nobody any longer dares to farm the valley, and everyone passing through gives a stone to the vile revenant's cairn in order to mollify her.

Into this valley moves a man named Bjartur, who has worked for eighteen years to raise the few crowns necessary to buy this land—the only land he can afford because no one else will have it. As he and his new wife pass the cairn on their way in, she begs him to give Gunnvor a stone. Though it causes her terrified agony, he refuses. He does not believe in ghosts—or to the extent that he does, he defies them. It seems ridiculous and heartless that not even for his superstitious wife's sake will the man give Gunnvor a stone: "Damn the stone you'll ever get from me." Of course, the man is so dirt poor that all he has is a stone, his idiotic indomitability, and his outdated poetry.

Sure enough, his wife dies during childbirth, terrified and alone. Years of bleak poverty later, Bjartur's second wife dies. But that is not all. His eldest son is taken, and like cursed animals in old Icelandic sagas, Bjartur's all-important sheep begin to turn up mangled, muti-lated, fiendishly murdered. What to do?

When the local farmers come together to talk things over, we get some of the funniest passages in the book. These people are as ignorant as rocks. They have never been out of their valleys; they are as innocent of nearly all human knowledge as the new-blown snow. When they gather we at first hear only chewing, slurps of strong coffee, burps, and grunts. Once they are lit up by six or eight cups of coffee, the conversa-tion begins. The scene reminds me of myself in company with other Civil War buffs, scholars, professors:

> The men sat down, produced their snuff-horns, and proceeded to discuss the weather with the deep gravity, the scientific restraint, and the pon-derous firmness of style with which this topic was always hallowed. A general review of the weather during the past winter was succeeded by a more minute analysis of the varying conditions of spring, with a com-prehensive survey of the lambing season and the condition of the sheep and the wool, followed in turn by an examination, week by week, of the summer. One corrected another, so that there was no lack of accuracy.[2]

After the sheep atrocities, a conclave of hardscrabble farmers de-cides to gather all the local men and women at the site of the recent bloody violence, and call in the local minister to deliver a few appropri-ate remarks. The event is well attended, of course. "People rarely show

such enthusiasm as when they are seeking the proof of a ghost story —
the soul gathers all this sort of thing to its hungry bosom."³

Hungry bosom indeed. This book reminded me of an incident that
took place the previous summer in Gettysburg. One night, filled with
thoughts of the dead, I had gone out to the battlefield. It had been
moonless and still.

I had been standing motionless — a behavior which might be considered a little peculiar, but any Civil War nut would understand. I suppose I had not moved for ten minutes. Among other things, I was
thinking how quiet and nice it was, except for the occasional helicopter
bug. I don't know what they're really called, but they come out of
nowhere with their low, throbbing buzz and invariably fly at your ear or
against your forehead or drop down between your collar and your neck.
These things are as big as .58-caliber bullets. I wondered when the next
one was coming. I was also thinking that I was completely alone out
there on the battlefield. I had a clear view of the field along Cemetery
Ridge all the way to the Round Tops and across the Emmitsburg Road,
and there was not a set of headlights in the whole expanse.

Aloneness, one can deal with. I walked a few steps, finally, then
turned to go back. It is being *not alone* when you expect to be alone that
is a problem. About thirty yards away stood a man. Silent as I had been,
I had not heard him. He was wearing what appeared to be tennis shoes,
a dark jacket, and a brimmed hat. Though I had moved, and was wearing khaki pants that were probably visible in the reflected light from the
town, he acted as if he had not seen me. Indeed, what he did, someone
would not do if he were aware of anyone watching. With complete
abandon, he leaned toward a regimental monument and embraced it
with both arms, then fell to his knees in front of it. He then got up
and went around to the side of the marker away from me, coming into
view again rather more slowly and perhaps more guardedly than I would
have expected.

Unusual behavior, especially when it appears to involve emotions,
is hard on Lutherans, and by this time I had had enough. I walked
toward the Visitor's Center, somewhat regretting that I had parked in
the lot there, instead of on the road here. He passed within about ten
yards of me going the other way, but I could not see his face. I would
have greeted him to get a response, but I did not want to embarrass him
(this is also very Lutheran), on the hopeful assumption that he was a
person. Also, I was uncertain as to the quality of my voice.

I don't know whether this is a ghost story. Ghosts don't wear tennis shoes — at least not Civil War ghosts. Or, I don't suppose they

do. In any case, that fellow should have had the decency to be aware of how briskly those books on the ghosts of Gettysburg are selling, before frightening a taxpayer. I remember thinking, well, here's someone for whom the War is more real than for me, and I thought *I* was excessive.

I turned (many times) to look at the figure (particularly, I must confess, to see if he was silently following me, on cat feet) but almost immediately I could not distinguish him from the background anymore. No figure. Nowhere. No sound. No footsteps . . . or — at about this point one of those helicopter bugs struck my ear and scared the living hallelujahs out of me. I swung at it — grateful, of course, not to have turned and found the man in the hat two feet from my face.

I got into my car. No one else was in it. I drove out of the lot, but something did not feel right. I did not want to get out of my car on Cemetery Ridge again. I was unsettled and things were wrong. What would I have seen, if I had spotted him again? A reflection of myself? What if he were a soldier? What if he *were* a ghost?

Let's assume what most of us think to be false, just to see whether we can learn anything by it. Let's assume that ghosts still haunt the battlefield at Gettysburg. It is not a pleasant assumption, as Laxness explains:

> Supernatural phenomena are most unpleasant for this reason: that having reduced to chaos all that ordered knowledge of the world about him which is the foundation a man stands on, they leave the soul floating in mid-air, where it does not rightly belong. One dare no longer draw any conclusion, even from the soundest of common sense, for all boundaries, even those between antitheses, are in a state of perpetual flux. Death is no longer death.[4]

Can we live with that assumption — that is, with its implications?

If there were ghosts, we might have been wrong about some things. We might have to admit that our perception of the universe is only partial at best, false and misleading at worst. If there were ghosts, our means and methods of collecting and verifying knowledge are incomplete: our scientific definition of what knowledge *is* would be eclipsed.

But that very definition prevents us from taking our assumption seriously. After all, we are only engaging in a "what if" exercise, far removed from the "hard history" in which we Civil War buffs are interested. But one ghost, *just one ghost,* would make our idea of "hard history" go *poof!*

Now, suppose we run into not some ordinary, haunted-house variety ghost, but a humdinger of a ghost, like maybe *George Washington*. Okay. On the way to Gettysburg it was rumored among some units marching at night that soldiers had seen the ghost of George Washington riding parallel to them. (To ask how they knew it was George Washington would be impertinent. If one sees the ghost of George Washington one *knows* it is George Washington. There is no possibility of confusing him with Elvis.)

You can imagine the tall man in Continental blue coat and light breeches, riding a spirited white horse. You can imagine him calling, as he did to his troops at Princeton, "Parade with me! Parade with me!" and riding that tall white horse right into the enemy's lines. If the Washington ghost rumor was an invention, what an invention!

It was, of course, most likely only a rumor meant to inspire the men, like the rumor that Little Mac was once again in command. But one cannot be sure. Imagine going into battle seeing ghostly ranks of Hitchcock's New England Continentals and the Green Mountain Boys and Washington's own Virginians, all at present arms as you pass them and move forward into the enemy's fire. What exhilaration! Just one little caution here, however. Again, Halldor Laxness: "Everything that one has ever created achieves reality. And soon the day dawns when one finds oneself at the mercy of the reality that one has created."[5] Those who play with war are playing with fire.

All of us create ghosts when we refight the Civil War. We make imaginary ghosts out of the hard history that we read. Once a ministerial student came across me as I stood on the Gettysburg Lutheran Theological Seminary grounds, looking across the fields toward McPherson's Woods. He observed with quiet amusement that every so often he sees one of us buffs just standing and looking. What do we do, when we're just standing there, he wondered. "We imagine," I told him. "We try to see it." We make ghosts.

It is strange that we believe in those phantasms more than we believe in the ghosts people swear to us they have seen in some house one night. Our phantasms are based on books like David Martin's fact-filled book on the first day at Gettysburg.[6] He tells us where each regiment was when, so we imagine the flags, the smoke, the cannons blasting, the crowded infantry fire sounding like sailcloth tearing, the regiments coming on and yelling, companies of men falling. The one thing we cannot imagine is what it means to be shot and killed in Civil War battle. Although we might be able to imagine what it was *like* to be shot and killed, we cannot imagine what it *means*. The ghosts could help us with that, even if we only assume the "what if" of their existence, even if we do not believe in them, for the concept itself of ghosts haunting the battlefield is very, very instructive.

George Washington does not haunt the battlefield, according to the stories collected by Nesbitt and others. The ghosts are slaving, horrified medics and the agonized wounded; they are tramping regiments marching in the night; there is a floating white form of a woman around Spangler's Spring, a young man trapped in a cellar, a boyish Confederate wandering in a house, and maybe a strange-acting man along the monuments of Cemetery Ridge. Why are they there, or why do we imagine them to be there?

They are exceptions, these hypothetical ghosts. One hundred fifty thousand men fought at Gettysburg and something like seven thousand died there. How many ghosts have been seen — that is, different ones? Maybe a few hundred. So perhaps 5 percent of the killed allegedly are ghosts haunting the battlefield.

Most of the dead are not only dead but gone — happily, perhaps. So maybe war *is* all right. You die in one and move on. You have done your duty and gone on to the next place, the next thing, if any. It's those 5 percent that are troublesome. They are really "poltergeists." When a great picture is slightly troubled, when something does not quite fit but nags and nags, you begin to catch the real vision.

Ghosts are said to haunt places when something has not been "resolved." For them, there is something wrong with this picture. They are troubled. It is the depth and length of their trouble that haunts and terrifies us. What horrible disturbance did they suffer, so that 140 years later they are still there, walking, standing, staring? What has reduced their ordered knowledge of the world? What is it that haunts them?

In the old Icelandic sagas the troublesome ghosts are not "resting easy." Such goings-on, or the imaginings of such goings-on, have not left the world's stage. Far from it. In Ibsen's great play, *Ghosts*, a young man becomes a ghost himself, an image of the destruction alive within his own body: his father's venereal disease racks the son, turning his mind to vegetable chaos. Things have not been as they seemed. The verifiable phenomena of the young man's life have not been real. The ghost is real, and it kills him. "The sins of the fathers are visited on the children," the young man realizes.[7]

There are consequences to what we imagine. In the case of Civil War buffs, we had better watch out. We have created a reality, and during much of our significant time we live in it. Whoever goes and lives in another reality needs to be careful. An alternative reality could contain health, and could contain danger. Probably some of both, which is why sanity is such a chancy construct. But it is not as if Civil War buffs need to be worried for their sanity (says one of them). They are a hale, solid, earnest, patriotic lot, often infused with the ideals of honor, freedom, courage, and devotion that were once carried by those heroes whom they study and imagine. It is these noble traits that inspire us and justify our obsession. But why are we obsessed? What in us is unresolved?

Who are the living, and who are the ghosts?

Perhaps it is more than the ideals, the drama, or the heroism of the Civil War that haunts us. Perhaps it is something at the bottom of the tragedy. The force with which we contend, and which we have not been able to shake off even after a hundred years, is the force of evil, the presence of evil, and, like the young man in Ibsen's *Ghosts*, we have it in us. Something is not right about this picture, as we look about us, and as we look into the past. Whether we know it or not, the ghosts are speaking to us.

Whoever that man was I saw that night on Cemetery Ridge, I frightened him as much or more than he frightened me: he lit out or hid without a trace. And I come back, I come back, I come back. In my mind I am still there.

Because of the ghosts we are led to question the basic ethos of the Civil War, as we do of all wars. We admire those soldiers of sunny 1861 for their devotion to duty; we lionize those survivors of dark 1865 for doing that duty for four long years in the midst of death, disease, cold, wet, hunger, loneliness, and terror.

Mrs. Alving, the mother of the disease-ridden young man in *Ghosts*, says,

> I can never be free of the ghosts that haunt me. . . .
> . . . I'm inclined to think we're all ghosts . . . it's not only the things that we've inherited from our fathers and mothers that live on in us, but all sorts of old dead ideas and old dead beliefs, and things of that sort. They're not actually alive in us, but they're rooted there all the same, and we can't rid ourselves of them. I've only to pick up a newspaper, and when I read it I seem to see ghosts gliding between the lines. I should think there must be ghosts all over the country — as countless as grains of sand. And we are, all of us, so pitifully afraid of the light.[8]

The minister to whom she has said this expresses amazement at her thinking, but she tells him it was he who caused her to see things this way.

Yes, when you led me back to what you called the path of duty and obedience — when you praised as right and proper something that my whole soul revolted against as an abomination.[9]

That is, we sometimes forget that the Civil War was a war. "War is all hell," Sherman said to his boys; that was a long time ago and we have forgotten. What is wrong with this picture? The Civil War was peopled by heroic characters, characters we love and admire. Like Mrs. Alving's son, they were brave boys, good boys — and some of their generals were noble and true, "manly" as used to be said — and they died, half of those who died, in one of the best causes ever fought for, and nearly all of them for honor, freedom, and justice as they saw them. Have not the country and our very lives been perfumed by their sacrifice? Is that sacrifice not as sweet and proper as any in the long, speckled history of humankind? But what is wrong with this picture? These brave boys killed each other; they did not merely clench their teeth and walk in to die, like Christians in the Coliseum. They perpetrated the dirtiest horrors and coldest brutalities of their age, on a scale yet unknown on this continent. Maybe it was not so sweet and proper. Maybe it was an "old lie," as Wilfred Owen wrote during the next great war:

> If in some smothering dreams you too could pace
> Behind the wagon that we flung him in,
> And watch the white eyes writhing in his face,
> His hanging face, like a devil's sick of sin;
> . . . My friend, you would not tell with such high zest
> To children ardent for some desperate glory,
> The old Lie: Dulce et decorum est
> Pro patria mori.[10]

War is a tragedy in which all are involved, and all are devoured. "My subject," wrote Owen, "is War, and the pity of War."[11] Innocence pairs strangely with guilt, honor with shame, the divine will with the worst that is in the human heart. What is good, and what is evil? What is life, and what is death? War drives these questions into our minds, and these questions remain unresolved. They haunt us, and if they do not haunt us, we are dead and need to be awakened.

Toward the end of *Ghosts*, the son says in pathetic bewilderment, "That's just what I simply can't understand. I've never led a dissolute life at all — not in any way."[12] Nor did those boys at Gettysburg lead lives of shabby dissolution, compared to what we might expect today. It was an age of innocence, an age of sentiment and sentimentality, and why, why, did Brother have to die? In no war within memory have so many brave and noble young men fought and maimed and killed each other.

The race, it seems, is not as innocent as we had thought. Ghosts — they strike to chaos all our ordered thinking. What is innocence, and what is guilt? If Brother died for someone's guilt, whose was it? Mine? His own? As Laxness seems to show us with his harsh Icelandic peasant, human independence requires a kind of hardness like a stone, a hardness that kills, a hardness that can defy and equal the worst atrocities inflicted on us by a vile, unresting spirit.

So these ghosts at Gettysburg have made chaos of the clearest boundaries that we thought existed. Death is no longer death. "What is death?" One of Laxness's characters asks, "And what is life?" What is innocence, and what is guilt? What is good; what is evil?

Ibsen's title in Norwegian is *Gegngaengerer* — those who return. The obscure English word *revenant* is the best translation. Like the evil spirits of Old Norse sagas, the young man in Ibsen's *Revenants* (*Ghosts*) is tortured by the evil within him. Are the ghosts at Gettysburg prophets, in the way Ibsen's play is prophetic? Maybe they are signs and signals of the very human essence of battle. Maybe they tell us that to die in battle means to be destroyed by the evil in all of us; and for some this evil cannot be shaken off, not after a hundred years. Time has no meaning; and what is life? Are we awake, or are these ghosts awake and alive, these revenants, these figments of our imaginations, these horrors of our dreams, these whispers and rappings in the night? Why do we sleep? Are our senses not awake? Can we not hear? Do we already have the dull, cold ear of death? Why do we not see them, these horrified prophets? Why do we not see ourselves?

Those Icelandic sheep farmers in Laxness's novel, after all, are no more stupid than we are. Their comic palavers lead finally to an understanding that strikes to chaos our ideas of who is wise, and who is foolish, what is cold, and what is brutish. A farmer explains:

> Now, one day in the summertime, shortly after war broke out, it so happened that I had occasion to visit the District Medical Officer on some small business connected with the animals' physic, and while we were sitting over a cup of coffee he brought out a most interesting foreign book and showed me some pictures of these two countries, France and Germany. I should like to make it clear that I examined the pictures as closely as circumstances allowed. And I came to the conclusion, after minute scrutiny and conscientious comparison of the pictures, that there is no fundamental difference between France and Germany at all, and

that they are actually both the same country, with not even a strait between them, much less a fjord. . . . That is why I have arrived privately at the conviction, and I am fully prepared to maintain it in public if need be, that the aforesaid disagreement between these men [World War I] sprang from a misunderstanding. And that the cause of it is that each thinks he is better than the other, when as a matter of fact there is no real difference between them except perhaps some trifling variation in the manner of wearing the hair. Each maintains that his country is in some way more holy than the other's, though in strict reality France and Germany are exactly the same country.[13]

And what happens if all those killed by each other go to heaven? A quaint idea, to be sure, but the "what if" is very instructive:

do they go on fighting with undiminished imbecility in heaven, and if so for how long? And if they murder one another afresh, where do they land then? Will there eventually arrive a time when the whole universe will be too small to accommodate people who want to murder one another in stupidity, for no reason and to no purpose to the end of all eternity?[14]

Finally the hero, or antihero, of *Independent People* not only gives the thousand-year-old revenant a stone, he has a headstone made for her. Why?

Some people said that she had killed folk, and who hasn't killed folk, if it comes to that? What are folk? Folk are less than the dirt beneath your feet when times are bad.[15]

The war has made Iceland prosperous. Europe wants her wool and mutton. Bjartur is no longer dirt poor. Killing might not be so bad. What is good? And what is evil? So he has the stone inscribed, "To Gunnvor from Bjartur."[16]

His surviving son (the oldest is dead, the youngest has emigrated) has inherited his father's indomitability, the glory of humanity in the face of the overwhelming numbers and resources thrown upon us by a hostile or perhaps indifferent universe. But he has inherited the father's disease also. What is the point, he muses,

of surrendering oneself to the power of nonsensical dreams, or even ghosts, as his brothers had done. And now of course they were both dead, each in his own fashion, whereas he was alive and the owner of six sheep.[17]

Who is dead, and who is alive? The sins of the fathers are in the children; they are the ghosts that haunt us; they are the revenants that come back, always come back, those pale few who are the unresolved evil in ourselves.

The ghosts we see are the ones who regret, and they remind us of what lies at the bottom of all war. Not heroism, but regret. If we cannot see them, it is because they are inside us. Maybe all we can do is laugh. How can we defy ourselves? This disease in us has enabled us to survive; it makes us mean and ridiculous—and it takes us far enough from ourselves to give us hope that in the end the psalmist was right: "Surely the wrath of man shall praise thee."[18]

These revenants have seen something it is not within their power to resolve. They have suffered something deeper than they have strength to bear or heal. They have done much worse than they can ever forgive themselves for.

Meanwhile, I hope they keep on troubling us, warning us, and reminding us, those ghosts. I hope they will never let battlefields become scenes of peace and resolution. May they mourn, brood, scream, stare, cry, lament; may they growl and mutter; may they implore and regret, regret, regret.

Ghosts are witnesses still sitting—like madam with her knitting, clicking out a long black shroud—though the years pass through the door. They appall our glorious dreaming, ridicule our epic seeming, point to all the pale souls streaming from the steaming fields of war, bound with agony and regret to their own old fields of war—moaning always, *Nevermore*.

The American Iliad

Some of us remember the two-volume set of photographs and first-person accounts, edited by two well-known historians, called *The American Iliad*. I suppose we could call the Civil War anything we want — "the American Odyssey," "the American Aeneid," "the American Dunciad" — but only if our title seems to fit and illuminate the war, will it wear well. If enough of us are willing to interpret the war along lines suggested by our figure of speech, the figure will endure and exert a shaping force on the historical imagination.

The *Iliad*'s subject is war itself. It describes war as wrath, or rage. Who can forget the famous opening, "Sing, Goddess, of the wrath of Achilles . . ."? In a more contemporary translation, it reads,

> Rage — Goddess, sing the rage of Peleus' son Achilles,
> murderous, doomed . . .
> hurling down to the House of Death so many sturdy souls,
> great fighters' souls, but made their bodies carrion,
> feasts for the dogs and birds,
> and the will of Zeus was moving toward its end.
> Begin, Muse, when the two first broke and clashed,
> Agamemnon lord of men and brilliant Achilles.
> (I, 1–8)[1]

These lines show us a good deal of the epic as a whole. It is a poem of double vision. War is glorious: its chief exponent, Achilles, is "brilliant" and the Greek expedition leader is no less than a "lord of men." The soldiers are "sturdy souls." But war is also inglorious: the great fighters become "carrion, feasts for the dogs and birds." They do not go to the Elysian Fields; not even brilliant Achilles escapes Hades—a grim, gray shadow world populated by what Achilles will call "the exhausted dead."

Achilles is the poem's ostensible hero, but he is also its villain. He is excellent above all mortals in his fighting ability—and also, we soon see, the most inhuman, insofar as "human" is a desirable category. When he kills the Trojan champion, Hector, Achilles seethes,

> Beg no more, you fawning dog. . . .
> Would to god my rage, my fury would drive me now
> to hack your flesh away and eat you raw . . .
> (XXII, 407–409)

This is a Greek epic written by a Greek for a Greek audience, but the hero which the poem forces into our sympathy is Hector, the Trojan. In the climactic fight, we hope against fate that Hector will win. Where Achilles is cruel, selfishly indifferent to his army's welfare, and antisocial, Hector is humane, concerned chiefly for his country and family (until the one time when the rage of battle, and the gods, make him rash), and the joy as well as the hope of his city. Hector stands for civilization, but Achilles is the barbaric, Bronze Age loner.

The opening lines show that the subject will be the raging actions of a human being. But all this is done to carry out the purpose, or "end," of the divine will. The poet could not compose his lines without the muse: she sings, he writes it down. The epic action begins when two men in the same army "clash"; but the parameters of this clash are circumscribed by the gods. The goddess Athena physically intervenes to prevent Achilles from killing the "lord of men."

In describing war itself, the *Iliad*'s double vision surprises us. It is the world's greatest war poem, and the world's greatest antiwar poem. War is fascinating. Homer needed no theme or subject in addition to war: everything else is secondary. The story is about heroic values in tension with civilized values; it is about honor, courage, love of family and friends, jealousy, loyalty, hatred, respect for enemies—all in the crucible of war, the irresistible fiery force that dominates and destroys all of them.

The *Iliad* understands that war is irresistibly spectacular. Its bronze helmets shine brilliantly in the Mediterranean sunlight, the golden shields gleam like suns, the bronze swords and spear points flash like meteors. Even the gods cannot be indifferent:

> ... nor did mighty Zeus for a moment
> turn his shining eyes from the clash of battle.
> (XVI, 749–50)

Down below, the heroes have gathered, not from Alabama, New York, Mississippi, Georgia, Minnesota, Maine, and Virginia, but from Thrace, Athens, Sparta, Ithaca:

> ... Tribe on tribe, pouring out of the ships and shelters,
> marched across the Scamander plain and the earth shook,
> tremendous thunder from under trampling men and horses
> drawing into position down the Scamander meadow flats
> breaking into flower — men by the thousands, numberless
> as the leaves and spears that flower forth in spring.
>
> The armies massing ... crowding thick-and-fast
> as the swarms of flies seething over the shepherds' stalls
> in the first spring days when the buckets flood with milk —
> so many long-haired Achaeans swarmed across the plain
> to confront the Trojans, fired to smash their lines.
> (II, 549–59)

The heroes of these armies are famous to us still: Lee, Stuart, Sheridan, and Grant; Odysseus and Ajax, Hector and Aeneas — and above them all, the raging storm Achilles. On the eve of battle, like stars sprinkled across that clear ancient sky, flaring and flaming — the watch fires of a hundred circling camps.

In the morning, though Achilles broods alone in his tent, the armies meet on the ringing plains of Troy:

> At last the armies clashed at one strategic point,
> they slammed their shields together, pike scraped pike
> with the grappling strength of fighters armed in bronze
> and their round shields pounded, boss on welded boss,
> and the sound of struggle roared and rocked the earth.
> Screams of men and cries of triumph breaking in one breath,
> fighters killing, fighters killed, and the ground streamed blood.
> ...

... the savage work went on, Achaeans and Trojans
mauling each other there like wolves, leaping,
hurtling into each other, man throttling man.
(IV, 517–23, 544–46)

The crash of war is like the roar of nature itself. Now it descends to the small, to the personal level. Homer shows us what it means for man to throttle man:

... his sharp spear missed
and he hit Leucus instead, Odysseus' loyal comrade,
gouging his groin as the man hauled off a corpse —
it dropped from his hands and Leucus sprawled across it.
. . .
    ... Incensed for the dead
Odysseus speared him straight through one temple
and out the other punched the sharp bronze point
and the dark came swirling thick across his eyes —
down he crashed, armor clanging against his chest.
(IV, 567–69, 578–82)

Homer shows us that it is not sweet and seemly to die in battle. The *Iliad* shows force to be unsentimental, dehumanizing, and ugly:

Ajax son of Telamon charging quickly into the carnage
speared him at close range through the bronze-cheeked helmet,
the horsehair crest cracked wide open around the point,
smashed by the massive spear and hand that drove it.
His brains burst from the wound in sprays of blood,
soaking the weapon's socket ...
. . .
    ... Ajax next —
with a lunge he stabbed Phorcys, Phaenops' warrior son
bestriding Hippothous' corpse — he ripped his belly,
smashing the corslet just where the plates join
and the bronze spearhead spilled his entrails out
and down went Phorcys, grasping, clawing the dust.
(XVII, 337–42, 359–64)

As a burly farmhand wielding a whetted ax,
chopping a field-ranging bull behind the horns,
hacks through its whole hump and the beast heaves up

then topples forward — so Aretus reared, heaving up
then toppled down on his back. The slashing spear
shuddered tense in his guts and the man was gone.
(XVII, 593–98)

The sharp stone crushed both brows, the skull caved in
and both eyes burst from their sockets . . .
(XVI, 862–63)

We are too familiar with Civil War horrors to need many remind-
ers. As in the *Iliad*, there are glorious sights, such as the one Maj. Gen.
D. H. Hill described before Turner's Gap, when he saw the "serried
ranks . . . 'terrible with banners,'" march out in column upon column,
bayonets reflecting the sun. But a few days later, at Antietam, the
enemies had met face-to-face and hand to hand.

> Barton Harter . . . was killed instantly when a shell crashed through his
> chest. William Haney had the right side of his skull smashed to frag-
> ments by a ball. . . . Albert Bryant received a disfiguring facial wound
> when a minie ball struck the right side of his face, fractured his lower jaw,
> cut through his tongue, and lodged in the angle of the left jaw.[2]

The last description brings to mind what Achilles' friend Patroclus does
to an enemy in the *Iliad*:

> Patroclus rising beside him stabbed his right jawbone,
> ramming the spearhead square between his teeth so hard
> he hooked him by that spearhead over the chariot-rail,
> hoisted, dragged the Trojan out as an angler perched
> on a jutting rock ledge drags some fish from the sea,
> some noble catch, with line and glittering bronze hook.
> So with the spear Patroclus gaffed him off his car,
> his mouth gaping round the glittering point
> and flipped him down facefirst . . .
> (XVI, 480–88)

A man becomes a fish, then a bloody mass of meat. We read about it,
imagining, in our easy chairs. Like the photographs of Gardner and
Brady, the *Iliad* brings war into our living rooms.

And what does war look like there? Its face is "courage-shattering
Death." (XVI, 494) It annihilates all the virtues, even the primary one.
We must remember some things about the *Iliad* before we make it into a

Hollywood spectacular. First, the cause of the war, while in the hands of
the gods, is ridiculous and ignoble. A goddess is jealous and angry; she
makes a young man steal a king's wife. The aggrieved king and his
brother raise armies and besiege the offender's city for ten years.

What is the quarrel that opens the *Iliad?* Agamemnon and Achilles
both want the same girl (Briseis). This is part of their debate, considerably beneath the level of Lincoln-Douglas:

> ACHILLES: My honors never equal yours . . .
> . . . back I go to Phthia.
> AGAMEMNON: *Desert*, by all means . . .
> I will never beg you to stay, not on *my* account . . .
> . . . I will be there in person at your tents
> to take Briseis in all her beauty, your own prize —
> so you can learn just how much greater I am than you.
> (I, 193–219)

These men are not five years old; they are grown up enough to pro-
nounce "Phthia." But we are not impressed by the elevation of their
motives. In battle the opponents sometimes taunt each other with long,
vaunting speeches. Homer is not a fool. He does not fail to realize
that civilized, humane virtues have gone by the board. That is exactly
the point.

The noblest of the heroes, Hector, goes out to meet Achilles, but
first says farewell to his wife and son. Homer quite deliberately makes
this the most touching scene of the entire epic. He includes an image
showing us how unnatural war is. As Hector reaches to kiss his boy, the
high-plumed, flashing helmet terrifies the child. Hector is not ashamed
to remove the monstrosity in order to comfort his son and take him into
his arms:

> . . . his loving father laughed,
> his mother laughed as well, and glorious Hector,
> quickly lifting the helmet from his head,
> set it down on the ground, fiery in the sunlight,
> and raising his son he kissed him, tossed him in his arms,
> lifting a prayer to Zeus and the other deathless gods . . .
> . . . So Hector prayed
> and placed his son in the arms of his loving wife.
> Andromache pressed the child to her scented breast,
> smiling through her tears. Her husband noticed,

and filled with pity now, Hector stroked her gently,
trying to reassure her, repeating her name: "Andromache,
dear one, why so desperate? Why so much grief for me?"
(VI, 556–67, 574–80)

After a few more words, they part for the last time, everyone knowing what awaits this father and husband.

Shortly thereafter, Hector's brother Paris, the boudoirist who started this whole mess, comes along to find Hector still standing there, gazing down the street where his wife and child have gone. We do not want this good and noble man to die. Homer has *made* us feel this way.

Then he chops Hector up in front of our eyes. The duel with Achilles is no Hollywood showdown. The last thing we would expect is for Hector's courage to fail, but it does. He sees Achilles running for him, and takes to his heels. We expect a clash of titans; what we get is two guys hot-footing it around the walls of Troy. And not for only a few seconds. They go four times around the city. The scene is ridiculous. They pant, they sweat, they keep going — and we paid good money for this.

Then Athena, a goddess who hates Troy, appears beside Hector, looking like his brother. She fools him into thinking that two of them can handle Achilles. Hector turns to face the big Greek, and *poof!* She is gone. Then *poof!* She's beside Achilles.

Keep in mind that except for his heel, Achilles is invulnerable. No fight against Achilles is a fair fight. He needs a goddess like the 1997 Chicago Bulls needed Wilt Chamberlain to take off his jacket and wade onto the court. Achilles is even wearing armor made by a god; quite a fashion statement. But Athena helps him anyway. She deflects Hector's spear, then when Achilles misses (oops!), she brings the spear back to him for another try. So up to this point Hector has been sold, cozened, and cheated. Achilles does not have to be excellent; all he has to do is show up. And then, there is no battle. The two men dash at each other and Achilles runs his spear through Hector's throat.

What was too ridiculous to be glorious now becomes despicable. Achilles refuses to send Hector's body back to his family. He stands over the great Trojan's corpse as the Greeks rush up — that is, the ancestors of Homer's audience:

And not a man came forward who did not stab his body . . .
(XXII 438)

Achilles is not finished.

> So he triumphed
> and now he was bent on outrage, on shaming noble Hector.
> Piercing the tendons, ankle to heel behind both feet,
> he knotted straps of rawhide through them both,
> lashed them to his chariot, left the head to drag
> and mounting the car, hoisting the famous arms aboard,
> he whipped his team to a run and breakneck on they flew,
> holding nothing back. And a thick cloud of dust rose up
> from the man they dragged, his dark hair swirling round
> that head so handsome once. . . .
>
> And now his mother began to tear her hair . . .
> She flung her shining veil to the ground and raised
> a high, shattering scream, looking down at her son.
> (XX, 465–74, 479–82)

Then at last Andromache, Hector's wife, hearing the wail and groan, comes up to the ramparts and sees the arrogant Achilles dragging her husband's naked body around the city.

Now, even if we had never thought that war is all glory, we have been shown that war is all hell. It has destroyed everything, including the only person in the story we have come to care about, and his family. Honor, courage, excellence, decency, humanity have been butchered and dragged in the dust. The only individual who seems to be enjoying himself is Achilles. During the next few days, whenever he feels down, whenever he feels blue, Achilles hitches up the team again and takes the body out for another spin. (The gods don't like this because it violates some rule or other and so they prevent Hector's body from decomposing.)

Achilles himself is war. He is a machine of rage. First Agamemnon enraged him into staying out of things and letting his comrades get slaughtered by the Trojans. Then Hector killed Achilles' friend Patroclus. It wasn't even Hector's fault. Patroclus was wearing Achilles' armor, so Hector went for him. *Got you at last! Whoops. Oh-oh.* And now this rage goes beyond any previous rage.

When Achilles returns to the battle, his presence has the effect of the war god himself. Even the cooks on the Greek ships run out to fight. Battle madness is on them all. It even affects Hector across the way, who despite his family's pleadings, waits for Achilles.

Achilles does a lot of killing before he gets to Hector, in the most violent passages of the story. Slaying and butchering, the mechanism drives on, all fury, "insane to hack flesh" (XXI, 38). No one can stand before him; all go down before the reaper: he grinds and storms and mashes everything to blood:

> Die, Trojans, die —
> till I butcher all the way to sacred Troy . . .
> (XXI, 146–147)

At the bank of the river Scamander Achilles — "the hero" Homer calls him there — slashes a Trojan —

> slitting his belly open —
> a scooping slice at the navel and all his bowels
> spilled out on the ground. . . .
>   And trampling his chest
> Achilles tore his gear off, glorying over him now:
> ". . . Nothing can fight the son of Cronus, Zeus,
> not even Achelous king of rivers vies with Zeus,
> not even the overpowering Ocean's huge high tides,
> the source of all the rivers and all the seas on earth
> and all springs and all deep wells — all flow from the Ocean
> but even the Ocean shrinks from the mighty Father's bolt
> when terrible thunder crashes down the skies!"
>   With that
> Achilles pulled his bronze spear from the river bluff
> and left him there, the Trojan's life slashed out,
> sprawled in the sand, drenched by the black tide —
> eels and fish the corpse's frenzied attendants
> ripping into him, nibbling kidney-fat away.
> (XXI, 203–30)

This is too much for the river god, who cries out, "I am filled with horror!" (XXI, 250)

In an extraordinary passage, Achilles now takes on the river itself:

> . . . Achilles the famous spearman, leaping down from the bluff,
> plunged in the river's heart and the river charged against him,
> churning, surging, all his rapids rising in white fury
> and drove the mass of corpses choking tight his channel,
> the ruck Achilles killed . . .
> (XXI, 264–68)

Achilles at last is pushed back, but

> Again and again the brilliant swift Achilles whirled,
> trying to stand and fight the river man-to-man . . .
> (XXI, 298–99)

Wave after wave breaks upon him, the river roils, foams, churns, but Zeus and his wife Hera come to Achilles' rescue, sending Hephaestus, the blacksmith of the gods, who runs up a roaring fire against the river. Clouds and jets of steam shoot upward. Now it is not merely Greeks versus Trojans, it is water against fire, fire against water. The elements themselves rage it out, and fire wins.

"Hephaestus—stop!" cries the river god. "Not a single god can stand against you" (XXI, 405–406).

War has entered our living rooms and it is terrifying. It breaks in, huge and savage, dripping blood, its blade sharp and heavy. We cannot stop it. It is like fire. Not even the gods can arrest it. Neither the decency of the moral universe nor the horror of the elements can turn it aside. It rages on and consumes all in its way. It will devour and enflame and destroy. It will not stop against any force or power in the world, but only when it has consumed itself and retires of its own running-down. But only temporarily.

War is the irresistible force. It may attract with its spectacle; it may transfix and fascinate. But it will overpower everyone and everything. It is nuclear, it is chemical, it is biological; it is rage, it is fury; it is unlimited violence. The power of the universe, Zeus, is violent too; the supernovas explode, the stars thunder their unimaginable furnaces into the speeding streams of space and matter, galaxies collide with immense conflagration. What hand and what art dare frame war's fearful symmetry?

When the fire burns past, the remains are black. The few survivors know only loss. The *Iliad* ends not as we expect, with the triumph of the Greeks, but with Achilles and Hector's father weeping. What a mess, what a horror, we have made! And now, because of it, everyone we loved is gone. We have only grief, despair, floods of tears, and our own deaths. Achilles is human again, as he was in the story's first pages. In between, rage had stifled humanity. Achilles will die soon after the fuel of his rage is gone, and he knows it. He will be shot in the heel from atop the safe walls of Troy, by none other than the boudoirist, an anti-climactic humiliation. The old man Priam, robbed of his dignity, will be butchered at an altar. His fear, that the dogs will feast on his genitals out in the ruined streets, will come to pass. War will use up this fuel. It will find other, and flare up again.

As Troy fell, so will Athens, so will Sparta; so will the great empire of Rome. It makes no difference. The causes of war are war's itself to choose: causes are only fuel, like the men who perish, like the women and children who go up in dark smoke. This is war; this is the American Civil War, seen in the face, seen in our living room. Insofar as the Civil War killed and destroyed more Americans and more of America than all our wars through Korea, it was most like the *Iliad*, the great story of all war. The Civil War's fire burned so high and so long because the country had abundant fuel — not causes or issues but people, plenty of them, and factories and railroads and horses and money. The god of war did not have to work on short rations.

But in another sense, the Civil War is not like the *Iliad* at all. Perhaps the Civil War was like the Trojan War in some ways, but the Trojan War was not the *Iliad*. The *war* is not the *Iliad*; the *poem* is the *Iliad*. An epic poem is peopled with heroes; the Civil War had its heroes, but heroes are not men on battlefields, they are written things. An epic has its journeys, its elevated language, its games, its battles, and its divinities. Most of all, an epic has its Homer. What immortal hand or eye will frame our war's fearful symmetry? What sinews and what art will choose the story of the Civil War? What names, unheard and heard, will strive with men and gods on the ringing fields of Gettysburg? Whose sorrow will make future generations weep — before they rise up and turn to wars of their own?

The gods watch all the carnage as we read it; then they turn to their affairs. Like us, they love the spectacle; they grieve for a few of the dead. War is rooted in them, as it is in us.

But we are placed within something larger than ourselves. Perhaps there is nothing more powerful than war, nothing that has more force — because force and power and war are one. But there is something larger than force and war.

The most elaborate symbol in the *Iliad* is the shield made for Achilles by none other than that blacksmith god, Hephaestus, who steamed the river. Many of us suffered through this pages-long passage in high school, wondering why we had to read this and when would Homer get on with it. The shield, of course, is the context for the *Iliad*. The scenes forged upon it by the blacksmith — crippled, as the poet is blind — give a place to war, but it is a small place:

There he made the earth and there the sky and the sea
and the inexhaustible blazing sun and the moon rounding full
and there the constellations, all that crown the heavens,
the Pleiades and the Hyades, Orion in all his power too . . .

And he forged on the shield two noble cities filled
with mortal men. With weddings and wedding feasts in one
and under glowing torches they brought forth the brides
from the women's chambers, marching through the streets
while choir on choir the wedding song rose high
and the young men came dancing, whirling round in rings
and among them flutes and harps kept up their stirring call —
women rushed to the doors and each stood moved with wonder.
(XVIII, 565–69, 572–79)

The other city is at war. Ares and Athena are depicted within its walls, but these two gods are small figures within the great expanse of the shield. More space is given to the city at peace, and to other scenes spread across the well-wrought bronze. There is a "fallow field, broad rich plowland" (XVIII, 629). A king's estate is described farther on, with harvesters working to bring in grain while others bundle it and still others make preparations for the harvest feast. "A thriving vineyard loaded with clusters" is filled with girls and boys. One young boy plucks his lyre

so clear it could break the heart with longing,
and what he sang was a dirge for the dying year,
lovely . . . his fine voice rising and falling low
as the rest followed, all together, frisking, singing,
shouting, their dancing footsteps beating out the time.
(XVIII, 664–69)

And then the smith forged a herd of cattle, and after that a meadow. On this meadow, "the crippled smith brought all his art to bear," for it is like a vision of heaven:

Here young boys and girls, beauties courted
with costly gifts of oxen, danced and danced,
linking their arms, gripping each other's wrists.
And the girls wore robes of linen light and flowing,
the boys wore finespun tunics rubbed with a gloss of oil,
the girls were crowned with a bloom of fresh garlands,

the boys swung golden daggers hung on silver belts.
And now they would run in rings on their skilled feet,
nimbly, quick as a crouching potter spins his wheel,
palming it smoothly, giving it practice twirls
to see it run, and now they would run in rows,
in rows crisscrossing rows — rapturous dancing.
A breathless crowd stood round them struck with joy
and through them a pair of tumblers dashed and sprang,
whirling in leaping handsprings, leading on the dance.
(XVIII, 692–707)

And finally,

. . . he forged the Ocean River's mighty power girdling
round the outmost rim of the welded indestructible shield.
(XVIII, 708–709)

War is a small scene in this context, the blind poet within the work reaching out to see the curve of space and time, the boundaries of the universe rounding on itself. War has its place, but that place is small. War destroys everything it comes near, but it cannot expand to fill the universe.

What hems it in? What keeps it within its place, short of self-immolation? Not force, not war. The gods themselves, who are power, have only a small place within it. Like space, war has its own curve. Power turns upon itself.

The Civil War can be understood only in the context of a larger world. The men came home, hitched their horses to the plows; they planted and they harvested. The women left the empty hospitals, decorated the graves, and told their visions to the future generations. Wars came and went. The race proceeds by love and day-to-day minutiae; and the wide world always blooms again in spring.

Only within its larger context will the Civil War be written for the ages. Only when its causes are seen to be the very things that we cannot explain, will the war's true cause be told. Only when the war's results become our freedom and our sorrow will this war become a war of heroes for the ages. No one will need to know their names. They might be Achilles and Hector, they might be Grant or Lee or Lincoln. They might be some sad name that rests beneath a weathered stone somewhere on a lonely hillside. But whatever the names, they will be yours and mine, and they must belong to someone whom a reader ages hence will recognize and know to be himself, and herself. The epic will unite the warring sides at last, because in poetry the past and future, the heroes and the hearers — all people everywhere — are one.

We are larger than war, or else we could not write about war. We are not fully deluded by power yet, or else we would not love what perishes. We are all one from age to age, or the epic song could not go on. We are all mortal men and women, else we could not sing the song of God.

The Song of God

Civil war is a perennial image of human nature. William Faulkner said that the subject of all literature is "the human heart in conflict with itself." "What makes a person commit evil against his own will?" asks the *Bhagavad-Gita*, while Saint Paul cries, "The good that I will, I do not; but that which I abhor, I do!"

As long as there is desire, there will be war, says the *Bhagavad-Gita*.

> Knowledge is obscured
> by the wise man's eternal enemy,
> which takes form as desire,
> an insatiable fire . . .
> (I, 39)[1]

The *Gita*, called the Gospel of Hinduism, is a war story. As in Homer's *Iliad*, the divine takes on human form, coming down among men on the battlefield.

The battle about to begin as the *Gita* opens is the great climactic battle of a civil war, the Gettysburg of India one might say. In fact, the *Gita* is set within the *Mahabharata*, a great war epic, the *Iliad* of India — but in the very midst of battle, the *Gita* rises above war, above time and space. It is called the "Song of God."

The human voice in the *Gita* belongs to a young prince named

Arjuna. At the beginning of the story, Arjuna faces the drawn-up array of the enemy, whose chariots, horsemen, and infantry confront the army of Arjuna and his brothers. A plain, soon to be a field of horrific carnage, separates the two forces.

> Conches and kettledrums,
> cymbals, tabors, and trumpets
> were sounded at once
> and the din of tumult arose.
> (I, 13)

It will be a battle of kin, a civil conflict. Those who lead one army are cousins of those who lead the other. The prince Arjuna commands his charioteer to drive out onto the plain so he can see both armies. The charioteer is Lord Krishna, the divine being, radiant in holy blue.

> "Krishna
> halt my chariot
> between the armies!
>
> Far enough for me to see
> these men who lust for war,
> ready to fight with me
> in the strain of battle."
>
> . . .
> Arjuna saw them standing there:
> fathers, grandfathers, teachers,
> uncles, brothers, sons,
> grandsons, and friends.
>
> He surveyed his elders
> and companions in both armies,
> all his kinsmen
> assembled together.
>
> Dejected, filled with strange pity,
> he said this:
> > "Krishna, I see my kinsmen
> > gathered here, wanting war.
> >
> > My limbs sink,
> > my mouth is parched,
> > my body trembles,
> > the hair bristles on my flesh.
> >
> > . . .

I do not want to kill them
even if I am killed, Krishna;
not for kingship of all three worlds,
much less for the earth!
. . .
Honor forbids us to kill
our cousins . . .
how can we know happiness
if we kill our own kinsmen?"
. . .
Saying this in time of war,
Arjuna slumped into the chariot
and laid down his bow and arrows,
his mind tormented by grief.
(I, 21, 22, 26–29, 35, 37, 47)

Like the *Iliad*, the *Gita* presents a supreme statement against war; but also like the *Iliad*, it shows war's attraction and inevitability. The *Gita* clarifies the nature of war, then rises above the battlefield as Krishna reveals the beauty of his divine nature.

You will almost always find flowers at the John F. Reynolds marker in McPherson's Woods, where the general was killed on the first day of the battle at Gettysburg. Who leaves them there? Sentimentalists? Women? Who cares enough about a Union general dead for 140 years to spend money for flowers? As if he will see them. As if his Dear Kate, whom he was to marry that summer, will see the flowers and take comfort in the honor, and in the honor see affection that perpetuates her own. Don't we know enough living people who need our flowers? Why do we spend them on the dead?

> "Civil War buffs" . . . are a remarkable phenomenon in American life. In-deed, they are unique, for no other facet of American history — not even the Old West — has attracted such a large constituency. They include the members of more than two hundred Civil War Round Tables in all parts of the country, an estimated 40,000 reenactors who don their replica blue or gray uniforms and take up their replica Springfield rifled muskets several weekends each year to reenact Civil War battles, the more than 250,000 subscribers to our popular monthly or bimonthly Civil War magazines, many of whom also buy millions of dollars of Civil War books

each year, providing the most faithful customers of the History Book Club and sustaining several publishing houses that specialize in reprinted and new Civil War books, and the network of collectors of everything from brass buttons and minie balls to Civil War paintings and prints.[2]

The Civil War is still alive because the country still celebrates a long, long funeral for its dead. The reenactments, conferences, articles, and books will often show a subtle quality of grief; but the battlefields, preserved in numbers and fervor unique in all the world, are the cemeteries, replete with markers, flowers, people asking why, and perhaps for some, the presence of the dead. A man I know who has lived in nearby Washington, D.C. for sixty years came for the first time to Gettysburg and said, repelled, that the whole place was "one damn cemetery." Some of us never notice it until an unbeliever offends us with a comment such as that. We never noticed it because we live there — in the sense that those deaths, those dead, have been essential to what we know as life. But for all that, the man was right: the place is one large cemetery. Our interest in the Civil War is one long funeral. It is not necessarily morbid to say so.

A characteristic of classic epics like the *Iliad* is games, particularly funeral games such as those that end Homer's story:

> Ready —
>   whips raised high —
>   At the signal all together
> lashed their horses' backs and shouted, urging them on —
> they broke in a burst of speed, in no time sweep the plain,
> leaving the ships behind and lifting under their chests
> the dust clung to the teams like clouds or swirling gales
> as their manes went streaming back in the gusty tearing wind.[3]
> (XXIII, 410–15)

After the chariot race, a boxing match. Then,

> Quickly
> Achilles displayed before the troops the prizes set
> for the third event, the grueling wrestling-match.
> For the winner a large tripod made to stride a fire
> and worth a dozen oxen, so the soldiers reckoned.
> For the loser he led a woman through their midst,
> worth four, they thought, and skilled in many crafts.
> (XXIII, 779–85)

Without comment, we pass to the footrace:

> They toed the line —
> and broke flat out from the start and Ajax shot ahead
> with quick Odysseus coming right behind him . . .
> (XXIII, 842–44)

All these competitions, and more, pass before the reader after the huge, elaborate funeral of Achilles' friend, Patroclus.

This strikes the contemporary eye as foreign — soldiers dressing up and passing in review, staging mock battles; competitions being held and prizes awarded. But what else are reenactments? Even conferences and articles sometimes take the form of competitions.

The Greek idea was not a morbid one; nor was it as frivolous as the modern word "game" suggests. Games were mourning in an elevated way, marshaling great human abilities to demonstrate the vigor of life. A funeral was a celebration. A higher than normal exuberance was expressed, to purge the grief among survivors and to honor the hero whose life was thereby celebrated more than his death was lamented. All die, but this one surely lived. Funeral games were also a celebration in the way a priest will "celebrate" the Mass. It commemorates a death, but its purpose is to instill life. Such games were "solemn" like the Mass — not meaning dreary or pretentious, but rather serious, deliberate, and in a way deeply appreciative, while possibly exhilarating. What could be more like a reenactment?

The leading element is Honor. Funeral games honored the dead. The skills of the living were harnessed, along with their highest emotions, as gifts for the dead — a kind of energy for them, a last devotion, a last attempt to give them something. No material gift will do anymore; instead we give of our time and energy — of our lives themselves — to buoy the dead up in passing to eternity.

The honor of everyone is at stake. To fail to celebrate seriously enough, long enough, elaborately enough, would bring discredit on the living. To compete with less than full acceleration would be to shame the living with the dead.

Honor — the intangible demand, the invisible necessity — moves it all. It also motivates us more than we know. In his book on the origins of war, Donald Kagan analyzes the Peloponnesian War, the Second Punic War, the First World War, and the Cuban missile crisis on the basis of Thucydides' three causes of armed conflict: fear, interest, and honor.[4] He finds that honor is far from obsolete in bringing people to battle. The lucrative sentimentality of contemporary funerals could not do without subtle appeals to honor. The dead seem to lay their claims upon us. To live without honor is virtually intolerable in much of civilization. When the Marines draw their line in the sand, the nation lines up and stands behind them for "duty, honor, country."

Among the many things the Civil War was fought for, honor must be placed near the forefront. Men enlisted for the sake of the South, and to defend Old Glory; and they continued to rally round their bullet-riddled flags in battle after battle. These men left their homes and families; they relinquished their lovers and friends; they became novitiates of hunger, fatigue, poverty, and death.

What is the link between honor and death? The two do not necessarily mate, but the essential pledge of honor is to sacrifice without reserve. For what? For immortality. One way or another, maintaining honor is to claim the imperishable. Whatever imperishables we seek, they can be held only by those who do not themselves die. Honor is a kind of integrity that our bodies cannot give us. It seems worth denying and defying the world for, because it represents a wholeness the world cannot provide. For honor, we will give up and deny what we love and whom we love.

Honor is a refined form of self-preservation. The quarrelers in the opening scene of the *Iliad* demonstrate this. They fight over a captive woman so that their honor is not sacrificed. Agamemnon is a king; to lose honor would be to lose his place, and discredited kings do not survive. On a higher level, Achilles must preserve his honor as the greatest fighter, because that is his basic identity. He will hold *himself* together. His integrity is partly composed of fame, his only immortality. Without his honor, Achilles would be nothing, now and forever; that is why he chooses to die early in battle rather than go home and live to an old age.

But looked at from the standpoint of behavior, honor is something for which people will die. People will die in love, and people will die in rage, but one of the few abstractions people will deliberately die *for* is honor. That is because honor promises us the only immortality we can reach for ourselves. But it fails us. If it turns to dust in our dying hands, it is because the kind of immortality we have bought is an extended ticket on the wheel of birth and death, as the *Gita* would phrase it.

As self-preservation, honor reveals itself as a kind of power. It is an insistence. It is the ultimate kind of force we can manufacture. So it must be a form of attachment. It is *desire* with all the human smell forged and frozen out of it. The person who dies for honor has given the only thing he had for the only thing he wanted. The *Gita* sees to the core of this economics of glory:

> Driven by desire, they strive after heaven
> and contrive to win powers and delights,
> but their intricate ritual language
> bears only the fruit of action in rebirth.
> (II, 42)

The wind of the spirit blows only where it wills, said someone often compared to Krishna. *If you would be born again, not in the flesh but in eternity, it is the spirit which must give you birth.*

"Do not grieve for the dead or the living," says Krishna. (II, 11) Arise, and do your duty:

> Impartial to joy and suffering,
> gain and loss, victory and defeat,
> arm yourself for the battle,
> lest you fall into evil.
> (II, 38)

The wars go on. Troy is still to be attacked and defended, the world must still be made safe for democracy, we have touched only the tentacles of tyranny. But still we linger behind and mourn the dead we never knew.

Or do we mourn ourselves? Are we still torn, like the country? Is the Civil War our own heart in conflict with itself? The Civil War buff tends to be uninterested in abstract historical theories and forces: he is interested in *the war*. It is the war, these battles, these maneuvers, these muskets — which killed these honored dead. But human beings are seldom compellingly interested in anyone other than themselves. If we stay on the old battlefields, it is because we are not finished mourning for ourselves. If we linger to ask "Why?" it is because we do not understand our fates. If the games go on, it is because we hope that honor assuages our own tragedies. The Civil War has entered our imaginations. There, it speaks face-to-face with our hearts; there, we see ourselves as we otherwise would not.

On the battlefield we are timeless. The breath of the eternal stirs in the soft rustle of leaves, supports the distant, casual flights of birds, rests upon us in fields now far from the madding crowd, makes an altogether different kind of sound in the heart:

Realize
that pleasure and pain,
gain and loss,
victory and defeat
are all one
and the same.[5]

There are answers on these battlefields, answers to questions we have hardly dared to ask. Like Nicodemus in the night we come, having slipped away from the world of every day — from the scorn and scepticism of the world that knows, at most, the world — and we ask with the innocence and trust of boys and girls: *How can anyone be born after having grown old?* This year I am older; one day I will come no more. Will I return to walk these fields again? What these fields of asphodel reply, we trust:

> *Never were you not, old soldier;*
> *never will you cease to be.*

The words are dreadful and terrifying; the words are sublime comfort. Again and again the old soldier rises in the race, thrusts his sword in blood, falls beneath plunging hooves, comes again with spring, year in, year out, when the wagon wheels turn again and once again men slog the mud. The universal soldier, carrying within himself the universal civil war — his visitation comes always again and never ceases, laying fire upon our hearts, crowding us along with him to stumble into machine-gun fire and lose our faces where the hot shells scythe us down: *I am wrath,* he cries, and we are rage. *Come awhile to hell, be perfume in its fire, do the things that you abhor, and die.*

And yet when spring returns, the fields are here. Wrath has perished with its victims; rage is extinguished with the hearts of those we love. We leave a flower. We understand. The story of power is sung not by muses but by men and women; but in the hearts that live and die and live again, the Song of God goes on forever.

Wilderness

Seventy-mile-per-hour winds and horizontal rain. The hurricane had made landfall last night and was now raging through northern Virginia. Our bus was filled with soaked people exhausted from being out in the open ten seconds. The big vehicle shook every time a gust slugged it. Through our rain-layered windows we saw traffic lights bobbing; some overhead signals lay flat on the streaming wind.

The weather service had issued warnings for twelve inches and flash floods. Last night, the televised satellite picture had shown the ocean blue being spun up and out into a spidery galaxy of gray. The tour bus was a tunnel: we could see each other's steaming raingear but it was colorless outside. The driver could barely make out the highway, and nothing else. When we left the parking lot, the only color we had seen was the Holiday Inn's United States flag — its cloth and cord and pole in a riot of agony.

Moving as slowly as a mule-drawn wagon, we felt our way in this universal blue whipped to gray, big tires gimpy on the highway which had become a slick river, hard and black and shut off from all the world.

On the way to the Wilderness battlefield we were to stop at the Chancellorsville/Wilderness Visitor's Center, to see the place where Stonewall Jackson had gone forward, then. And when we stepped down off the bus it was dead calm. No wind; no rain. This was the past. This still spot was *long ago*.

A year before the Battle of the Wilderness, Lee's Army of Northern Virginia had fought the Army of the Potomac here, in this same tangled territory of scrub oak and vines and swamps and saplings, at what we call the Battle of Chancellorsville. But it was all one wilderness. As we stood in the soaked grass looking at the place where Jackson had been shot by his own men, a little rain began to fall again. Nothing dangerous, just a little *pat, pat, patter.*

Here is where the storm broke on Howard's 11th Corps: first a little murmur in the twilight, then a strange comedy of deer and rabbits bolting through the woods toward the relaxing soldiers, then an obscure *yip, yip* — then the Rebel Yell a mile wide and wilderness deep, gray and butternut men crashing through the brush in solid lines farther than you could see.

Major General Oliver O. Howard had been warned, but he never was willing to accept blame for his corps being surprised and routed. Rather than that, he would blame his men — a particularly unpleasant revelation about a general called "the Christian Soldier." Howard was a man you could love to hate, if the possibility of deep-seated hypocrisy still has any power to excite. He was nice, on the superficial level — the only general, one orderly said, who would actually thank you for holding his horse. A soldier who served under him later, during the Indian Wars out West, wrote:

> I remember him most for his ever-friendly speech, and his quiet manner. I don't believe I ever saw or heard of his being in a controversy. . . .
>
> Yes, Brigadier-General Howard was always as courteous to a corporal or a sergeant as he was to a major or a colonel, and those under him liked and respected him for it. Always kind and thoughtful, he was everything a man and an officer could be.[1]

This is the same Howard who was later called "the hero of Gettysburg" for choosing the defensive position that won the battle. That he deserved the honor is doubtful, but he was very careful about his prerogatives and reputation. That his poorly handled corps was responsible for the near-disaster at Gettysburg escaped his notice. Once again, as at Chancellorsville, his corps crumbled quickly — isolated units putting up strong defense while others melted. A New Englander, Howard probably did not respect the German contingent, which made up about half of the 11th Corps, and they had no affection for their teetotaling general either. In the 1st Corps, the Iron Brigade's German immigrants fought heroically — but their general, John Gibbon, respected his men and knew how to handle volunteer soldiers. Of course, he probably was not as polite as Howard.

Interestingly, Howard attributed the defeat at Chancellorsville to commanding general Joseph Hooker's impurity — not to his own ineptitude. The defeat was certainly of moral origin. Hooker had not lost the battle when he retreated; he had lost only some of the 11th Corps. Lee was about to attack Hooker's entrenched lines, something Hooker had originally wanted and which most likely would have resulted in an appalling repulse for Lee, like the ones at Malvern Hill and Gettysburg — but Hooker lost his nerve. Perhaps that was impurity.

Hooker was sent a little ways west, and did fairly well fighting under Grant and Sherman. Howard, after the war, was sent a lot farther west. It was Howard who closed the trap on Chief Joseph and the Nez Perce, way out in Montana, a few miles short of the Canadian border.

Howard had been in on the beginning of the Nez Perce War, too. His had been the task of ordering the Nez Perce off their lands onto a small reservation. He failed as a diplomat and as a boss, though others might have done still worse or simply murdered the Native Americans at the start. That's the trouble with Howard: you don't know what to think of him. His decency was such that Chief Joseph himself was reconciled with him years later. But perhaps a more implacable enemy the Native Americans could not have had. As a Christian fundamentalist, Howard might have seen the war against Native Americans as Israel against the Philistines, and as the Church against the heathen. You must act decently toward them, but there is no question — never the least question at all — as to what was what, or what should be what.

In a wilderness of trees and mountains up near the Canadian border out West in the decade following the Civil War, Chief Joseph and his Nez Perce waged a campaign more astonishing than Stonewall Jackson's in the Shenandoah Valley in 1862. Sometimes battling at ten-to-one odds, bringing their women, old people, and children with them, the Nez Perce fought the U.S. Cavalry eleven times, five of them being pitched battles — losing one, tying one, winning three. They marched eighteen hundred miles, not in the pleasant Valley of Virginia but in the Valley of the Bitterroot, and across the mountains. Unlike Stonewall Jackson, Chief Joseph did not win his campaign. Within a few miles of the border, he was cut off. This time Howard was not the patsy. This time the brilliant tactician had lost. John Gibbon, who had moved from the Iron Brigade and commanded a division at the Wilderness, commanded one of Howard's contingents in the tracking down and surrounding of the Nez Perce. This time, apparently, these two generals had defeated the wilderness, and those who belonged to the wilderness.

Before the Nez Perce War, Joseph had told Howard that he did not want houses, churches, schools, and gardens. "The Earth is our Mother," he had said. "Do you think we want to dig and break it? No indeed! We want to hunt buffalo and fish for salmon, not plow and use the hoe." Howard had called Joseph's statement "strange." But we remember Joseph's words, not Howard's or Gibbon's, though those two soldiers fought in a war which was about freedom:

> Let me be a free man — free to travel, free to stop, free to work, free to trade where I choose, free to choose my own teachers, free to follow the religion of my fathers, free to think and talk and act for myself — and I will obey every law, or submit to the penalty.[2]

When Chief Joseph died on the reservation, the white physician said he had died of a broken heart.

Joseph's surrender speech is more widely remembered than General Lee's farewell address. It has the plainness and honesty of Grant's manner of speaking. "Tell General Howard I know his heart," it begins. What did he know? What is in the human heart that defeated even the most brilliant general — more brilliant than Grant or Lee or Jackson — a war chief who knew better than anyone the ways of the wilderness: What did Joseph read in the human heart? "The little children are freezing to death," he said. The wilderness had stopped him.

> Hear me, my chiefs. I am tired; my heart is sick and sad. From where the sun now stands I will fight no more.[3]

He knew what was in Howard's heart: wilderness was in that heart. Joseph had fought it and lost.

But to Howard, Native Americans were wilderness. They were raw material for civilization, as their military ability above all else had demonstrated to the general. Like the virgin oaks and the iron ore around Spotsylvania, they could be put to better use than simply being left to flourish unseen. Thinking to be fair-minded, and meaning to give Chief Joseph's band their due, Howard concludes his written account of the Nez Perce campaign with these words:

> What glorious results would have been effected could these non-treaties ["non-treaties" being Howard's term for Joseph and his Nez Perce] have received the same direction [i.e., religious instruction] that the worthy missionaries were, in early days, able to give to the remainder of their

tribe, and have shown the same ability and persistence in peace that they did during the fearful Indian war. Certainly it would be gratifying to me, at any time, to see the remnant turn from savagery to civilization. They are a people, even in their wildness, picturesque and replete with interest. May not these, in the far-off Indian Territory where they have been sent, have a portion in the labor and the comforts of the world's progress.[4]

Chief Joseph knew this man's heart, all right.

The Nez Perce were simply the wrong people, "impure" as well as wrong, perhaps — just like the Germans under Howard's command here at Chancellorsville. And Stonewall Jackson, fighting his own mission against the wrong people, and to keep other wrong people in their place, surprised Howard right at the spot we were all surveying in the increasing drizzle. In this fight of Christian Soldier against Christian Soldier, the Christian Soldier lost. It will happen every time.

But Jackson lost his arm, and then his life. The victory at Chancellorsville, Lee said, was "dearly bought" at such a price. Militarily, Jackson was a man without illusions, but like Lee he was a genius at prestidigitation, able to inflict upon his enemies first illusions, then death. A year later, Lee could have used someone as good at illusion as Jackson was. Even at Chancellorsville, after Jackson's successful flank attack on Howard, the battle got pretty real for the Confederates and was almost lost the next day.

May third at Chancellorsville was the second-bloodiest day in American history, after Antietam. Lee's army tried grimly to connect its two wings, Hooker's army fought desperately to prevent it. The dense undergrowth roared and smoked, filled with howls and curses and shrieks hour after hour, until Confederate artillery finally got a commanding position and destroyed the center of Hooker's line. With the Chancellor House — Hooker's headquarters — crumbling in spectacular flames, Lee rode among his troops as the Confederate lines closed the deadly gap. And then other fires started. Artillery shells and rifle fire had lit parts of the woods, and wounded men who could crawled desperately until consumed by flame.

The thought of that day and what had happened there made me angry again in the increasing rain. A friend — well, let's say a colleague, now — had tried to tell me that the Civil War had been a relatively tame affair. All week before my departure on this tour, we had been in an E-mail debate over Ernest Hemingway, with whom my friend identified and who I suggested was a posing suburban whiner. He — my friend — had E-mailed from his suburb that Hemingway had shown us that such words as "duty," "honor," and "in vain" were empty words, hypocritical and manipulative. I said Lincoln and the Civil War were about such words, which are not empty words when good people fill them. He countered with an ignorant slur on "preachers" who have always been against Hemingway. He followed up by stating that next to the war Hemingway knew (World War I), the Civil War had "comparatively few casualties."

This needs a little correction, I banged on my keyboard. *In the Confederacy, 25% of eligible white males died in the war. The overall death rate of 4% is higher than for any World War I country — check James M. McPherson's* Drawn with the Sword.

Yesterday he answered. Facts did not turn him from his point of view: "There were more deaths in WWI — 62 million."

Who told you that? I replied interlinearly. *The total for WWI was under 20 million; even WWII was only 55 million.*

"A WWI battlefield was a far more dangerous place than a Civil War battlefield."

Total rubbish.

"Advances in technology made deaths more frequent and wounds more horrible."

If you factor in technology, you have to factor in medical technology.

I had considered not fighting this argument, but what is a friendship worth that requires such restraint? Bah! Humbug! Self-worth demands that you do not submit to every outrage. I added: *If the Civil War 12 lb. solid shot and .58 caliber soft lead bullet are not enough, go back to the Punic Wars and see if older warfare was less deadly or less horrible than your and Mr. F. J. Hemingway's favorite war. Consider Cannae.*

When confronted by willful stupidity you have to use overwhelming force. At Cannae, Hannibal's army had double-enveloped a Roman army of seventy thousand men and hacked them down to the man. If my acquaintance did not know that either, he could look it up.

We hurried to get back on the bus. The storm was now loosing a volley of shapeless bullets — one might say from all directions except that in this wilderness there were no directions. The rain had mushroomed into an ionic cloud of wind-hardened projectiles. Suddenly, running toward the exhaust of the bus, we were enveloped by an atmospheric swell. It was an airy force but iron gray, and you could see nothing. You could not differentiate any sound or color or degree of brightness. You just followed the ones ahead of you.

The rain became driving and heavy. Just as we turned off the highway to enter the Wilderness Battlefield, I saw a convenience store sign that said, "This is the end of civilization." We drove up the road and the forest closed in. Hat brims and ponchos flying, we got out and ran for the Park Service shelter at Saunders's Field, where the Battle of the Wilderness had started. Grant had crossed the Rapidan with an army of 120,000 men in four large corps, with cavalry, artillery, and an endless wagon train. Split into three corps separated to find food and forage, Lee's army waited with sixty-two thousand men, plus his thousands of auxiliaries. Both Grant and Lee miscalculated; each general underestimated the other. Grant thought Lee would not be able to fight him so soon after crossing, and Lee did not expect Grant to drive straight into the Wilderness and so started to advance and concentrate his corps nearly too late. Both failed to use their cavalry properly, and so neither knew where the other was.

When you look up the road passing through Saunders's Field, you are amazed at Robert E. Lee's nerve, coming right up to Grant and hitting him directly, with so many fewer men. One of Lee's generals called him "the most belligerent man in the army." But although Lee said he wanted to bring Grant to battle as soon as possible, he wanted to get his army's three corps together first, so as not to have them destroyed one by one. So this bold encounter was an accident. Since there was no cavalry buffer, Lee's 2d Corps, under Richard Ewell, had marched right up against Gouverneur Warren's 5th Corps (U.S.), and the two were already fighting across Saunders's Field and on a widening front into the dense wilderness on both sides.

Lee was in trouble. His 3d Corps, under A. P. Hill, was marching toward Grant on a road parallel to Ewell's but separated from Ewell's corps by almost two miles of scrub forest through which you could not see farther than fifty yards. Worse still, Longstreet's 1st Corps was way behind the rest of the army and would not be up until that night or maybe later. Lee's fight had started too soon.

For Grant, the sooner the better. Surprised but not alarmed, Grant ordered the rest of his army to stop its march through the Wilderness and turn on Lee. Then he had the order passed down to the 5th Corps to start fighting right away, never mind about getting things orderly — just "pitch in." But Warren was too experienced to throw his men against Robert E. Lee without first properly arranging lines of battle and getting more of his corps to the point of combat. He delayed the attack but could not resist peremptory orders for long, and so threw his men into battle. For a while, it seemed he would shatter Ewell's line.

In the pouring rain, we decided to delay the walk through Saunders's Field until after lunch. We got on the bus and went back up the road to look at the unmarked place in the woods where U. S. Grant had made his headquarters. The trees gave us some shelter as we trooped into the woods and then stood around the spot thinking.

Ulysses S. Grant came to be known as a "butcher" who threw overwhelming numbers of troops at the enemy in frontal assaults until he won a war of attrition. But that characterization of Grant is false. You can reach this conclusion in more than one way. You can compare Grant's Virginia campaign casualties — huge, admittedly — to the casualties incurred during the two preceding years at the Peninsula, Manassas, Fredericksburg, Chancellorsville. All of that fighting failed, but Grant's, which succeeded in eleven months, actually cost fewer casualties all told. It is true that his Virginia campaign cost more than any one of those previous battles, but the facts were that one battle would not defeat Robert E. Lee.

Another way to evaluate the "butcher" charge is to compare Grant's frontal assaults against fortified positions to Lee's. Grant did it at Cold Harbor and later said he regretted having done it. Lee did it at Malvern Hill, Gettysburg, the Wilderness, and would have done it at Chancellorsville. They all were like Cold Harbor, and they were not successful.

A third way to evaluate the "butcher" idea is to look at Grant's earlier campaigns. You will find maneuver, persistence, originality, and strategic brilliance, but not massive frontal assaults on fortified positions.

But should Grant have defeated Lee in one battle, thereby forcing an end to the war? Hooker had almost done it a year earlier, it seems. It almost happened on the second morning at the Wilderness, though quite possibly the Wilderness itself would have stopped the Army of the Potomac from exploiting a Confederate defeat. At any rate, destruction of the Army of Northern Virginia did not occur, and we have only actualities with which to speculate: Grant had to beat Lee the only way anybody had figured out to do it. The North could have quit instead of fighting it out, but chose to stick with Lincoln and Grant's "arithmetic."

One inevitably compares Grant to Lee. That Lee lost does not decide the question for Grant because of two things. Lee actually fought Grant to a stalemate in the summer of 1864, and Lee had far fewer men, guns, horses, and supplies than Grant. As Stonewall Jackson marched around Hooker's flank the year before at Chancellorsville, someone mentioned Hooker's having to protect large supply and ammunition trains. "I would like to have that problem," Jackson said, adding that the Army of Northern Virginia had never had enough men to throw into a victory to make it decisive. Now suppose Lee had Grant's problems: all the guns in the world, manned by excellent crews and supplied with better quality ordnance than CSA stuff; plenty of well-mounted cavalry; long, long supply trains; and 120,000 men — some veterans, some recruits and draftees.

Lee made an army of virtually uniformly high quality out of the Southern brigades he got in 1862, and perhaps he would have overcome the Potomac army's problem of inexperienced recruits and uncommitted draftees, bounty-jumpers, and end-of-enlistment troops as well. With all the other advantages, would he not have made short work of the war? It certainly seems that he would have. Lincoln was undoubtedly right to offer Lee command, back when the war was beginning.

But this hypothetical reasoning must encounter one reservation. If you are making a comparison by putting Lee at the head of the Army of the Potomac, you have to put Grant in command of the Army of Northern Virginia. Suppose on his drive south, Federal commander Robert E. Lee would not encounter Joe Johnston, Braxton Bragg, or even the brilliant P. G. T. Beauregard. Suppose it was U. S. Grant.

Would Lee have rolled over Grant? Military historians seem to agree that Lee was a better tactician than Grant, but Grant was the better strategist. Suppose instead of countering Lee tactically on the battlefield, Grant tried countering Lee strategically. Lee had at first countered McClellan's immense and growing Peninsula army strategically by sending Jackson up the Shenandoah Valley to threaten Washington. What would Grant have done?

William T. Sherman probably knew Grant best and might have had the clearest view of Grant's abilities. Give Grant equal numbers, Sherman said, and he will win. This might lock the case against Grant, but again there is a reservation. Numbers are equal only when the tasks are equal. Sherman said Grant needed two to one odds in 1864 to be even. Grant and Lee had different objectives. Lee had to survive; Grant had to win. To win, Grant had to conquer a territory larger than Napoleon's Europe. And he had to show results before the clock ran out. The clock would strike in November, when the election came.

Again, Grant's success was strategic. He did not defeat Lee on the battlefield. He lost nearly as many men as Lee began the 1864 campaign with, and he had not destroyed Lee. But neither had he retreated. The opposing armies had fought to a tactical stalemate in Virginia by midsummer. But Grant had sent a superior general with superior numbers against the Southern army defending Atlanta, and when the back door of the Confederacy was kicked in by Sherman, the North understood that the Confederacy was not going to survive. The strong man had come, bound up the owner of the house, and now the goods would be plundered. As one of the Army of the Potomac's soldiers said when Grant came to the field, "We felt that the boss had arrived."

It took both Grant and Lee to make a Wilderness. "Seven-eighths of the history of war is psychological," says Fuller.[5] For Lee, victory was not enough. He needed to destroy the Army of the Potomac, because for Grant, defeat was not enough. Grant's state of mind at the end of two days of Wilderness fighting was the decisive matter, just as Hooker's state of mind had been decisive here a year earlier. Lee had in effect driven Grant from the Wilderness by the evening of May 6. The integrity of Lee's line and Grant's failure to pierce the Confederate center had allowed the Army of Northern Virginia to seize and hold the Chewning Plateau, an elevated clearing dominating the centers of both armies' lines. Placing artillery there, the Confederates could have done to Grant's line what they had done to Hooker from Hazel Grove the previous year. But would Grant consider himself defeated and retreat, as Lee expected?

Lee had always worked upon his opponents' minds. He had intimidated McClellan, baffled Pope, and by concealment and audacity had become the nightmare that exposed Hooker's psyche. Having fewer resources, Lee, like Jackson, relied on illusion — *surprise, mystify, confuse*, Jackson had phrased it. Lee's victories were a pale horse that rode through Union generals' minds. He had deluded them into thinking his numbers were greater than theirs, that he could move faster than they could, that he could appear on either flank or in the rear at will, that he always had an unanticipated stroke to spring. But here on this knoll in this patch of woods, an officer comes to Grant, who sits whittling and smoking, and declares that Lee has again surprised them, that Grant had not known "Bobby Lee." And Grant, for one of the few times in his life, shows aggravation. He stands up and says, "Oh, I am heartily *tired* of hearing about what Lee is going to do. Some of you always seem to think he is suddenly going to turn a double somersault, and land in our rear and on both of our flanks at the same time. Go back to your command, and try to think what we are going to do ourselves, instead of what Lee is going to do."[6] What shall Robert E. Lee do now, now that he has met a man with no illusions?

Grant simply understood the nature of Civil War battle as few others did. In the evening of the second day, officers arrived to report that their entire right flank had been crushed, the 5th Corps routed. (An evening attack by two Confederate brigades had forced back two exposed Union brigades, but the small offensive had petered out in the darkness and the woods.) Some were saying that the left flank had caved in also. And Lee's frontal assault had plunged through the Union center. But Grant understood that in this war it was virtually impossible to destroy an army in good condition. He smoked a lot of cigars and whittled his gloves to threads, but he did not believe that he was enveloped or pierced. His numbers, his solid organization, and the Wilderness itself would prevent it. In this war, Grant realized, a man is beaten when he is convinced he is beaten. Grant was not convinced.

An army with its organization intact, with superior numbers and plenty of supplies and ammunition, had no excuse for retreating. Having a flank turned or being forced out of a position does not mean you lose. Lee understood that Grant's predecessors did not know this. What despair must have washed over him when he realized what Grant knew. That he kept fighting, and successfully, is a measure of his greatness; it was a moral greatness. Lee now knew that Longstreet had been right about Grant: "That man will fight us every hour of every day until the end of the war." And General Lee would fight back every hour of every day, until the end of the war.

Two indomitable human wills clashed in the Wilderness, and the Wilderness won.

What Lee had said about Meade at Gettysburg was even more true about Grant in the Wilderness: "We must whip him or he will whip us." Grant's continuing attacks on the first day in the Wilderness were meant to pin Lee's elements as they came up, preventing them from joining. Meanwhile Grant would drive his reserve corps through a gap between them. The plan should have worked. But even before it had failed for certain, Grant had shown Lee how the rest of the war was going to be run. Perhaps that is why Lee tried that last frontal assault: he knew it was the last chance. For good reason, Confederate veterans looked back on the Wilderness as their final opportunity.

But how real was the opportunity? You might sum a large part of Grant's character and abilities up under his ability to *concentrate*. A few days after the Wilderness, Grant was sitting on a fallen tree writing a dispatch as some Wisconsin troops were passing. A shell flashed "directly in front" of Grant, ripping fragments through the column and all around Grant — who "looked up from his paper an instant" and then went on writing. As the regiment put itself back together and resumed its march, one Badger was heard to remark, "Ulysses don't scare worth a damn."[7] He was concentrating. He sat and *thought* until he saw it; then he did it. "He talked less and thought more than any one in the service," said a member of Grant's staff.[8] The clarity of language in his orders, their directness and force, was a result of this concentration. Likewise, his lack of vanity and the absence of rancor showed that he was not tempted by distractions. He had a job to do and he purposed to do it. He would "fight it out on this line if it takes all summer." He was the perfect model of unattachment.

His strange tendency to disappear in crowds might have resulted from his refusal to try to be Somebody. The most famous man in the Union, Grant took the train to Ohio to visit his father. At the station, people waited and a man with a buggy was ready. The driver returned to Jesse Grant without the general. Must not have been on that train. Some time later, U. S. Grant appeared on foot. He had waited at the station until the crowd had dispersed, found nobody to give him a ride, and walked home. When he came to Washington in March of 1864, the Hero of the West and already the greatest celebrity that the North had produced, the city was prepared to give him a tumultuous welcome. A small, seedy-looking man with a boy appeared in the lobby of the Willard Hotel and asked for a room. This was a busy time; the best the clerk could do might be a room on the top floor. The man with the boy said that would be all right and signed the register. The clerk spun the book to write in the room number and read: "U. S. Grant and son, Galena Ill" — words he never forgot.[9]

Perhaps a similar shock of recognition passed through the Confederate army in the Wilderness. At any rate, this slight, quiet man who was unaffectedly plain wore an expression on his face like he was about to drive his head through a brick wall: a job was a job, and duty was duty. Lee would do his duty, too: if Grant wants a wall, then we shall be that wall. Surrounded by ragged and hungry soldiers, backed by an ineffective war government, his command structure in tatters, and faced by a determined and able foe who understood what needed to be done and how to do it, Robert E. Lee prepared for the greatest and hardest campaign of his life. "We must all do more than formerly." Necessity meets necessity, here in the Wilderness of Chancellorsville and Spotsylvania.

This morning at breakfast I had thought about Lee and Grant. Actually, to identify with a famous figure one studies is natural. I would not fault my earnest friend for identifying with someone per se, but rather for the man he has chosen to study and identify with. For myself, I find Grant to be by far the more likeable person, compared to Lee. Be that as it may, however, I have always felt more like Lee. The restaurant began to fill up around me. As I waited for a waitress, I reflected on what there was about Lee for which one might feel an affinity. He had a temper, that is true, but he held it under control. He was human, and not a mere statue. I looked at my watch; we were to leave in twenty-five minutes — still sufficient time. Lee's *presence* was something we have little awareness of today. But in the Widow Tapp's field on the second morning of the Wilderness, Lee's appearing at a moment of crisis turned calamity into victory. I watched the people at the other tables enjoying their breakfasts. Perhaps Lee was worth a whole division, just by his presence. Fifteen minutes remained for someone to take my order and bring it. I feel I look more like Lee, being tall rather than short like Grant. I think there is also something about my bearing. Ten minutes. Lee was dignified but gracious. Your gaze naturally would have been drawn toward him. There were eight minutes left. I stood up directly in front of a waiter and made my request. Though my beard is a Grant-style beard, I think facially I resemble Lee. The waiter repeated "that guy over there" to a waitress and a minute or two later she came toward me with a tray. All the other people had gone. I ate it fast — something small, I don't remember what it was — and then bolted toward the door, grabbing my old rain jacket around me. I think another thing about Lee was that he had an extraordinary ability to deceive himself.

So much for Grant and Lee: We began to file through the wailing woods toward the bus. It was about lunchtime and we would take shelter in the old Lacy House, which had been there during the battle and figured prominently in the minds of many 5th and 6th Corps men. In fact, the house had existed long before the battle.

Fortunately one of our guides worked for the Park Service, because the house was closed for restoration work. Inside, bare lath and plaster stood where wall surfaces had been torn out, and some room partitions consisted only of the old wood supports, interspersed with new ones. The floors were a mess of tools, sawdust, debris of all kinds.

A big cooler was brought in, along with sagging cardboard boxes filled with bag lunches. We drifted through the ramshackle ancient rooms and settled into wet corners with our lunches — not hardtack and coffee but sandwiches of some kind, bags of chips, apples, and cans of artificially flavored chemicals. The exposed bricks had been where they are now at the time of the battle. The floors were the same wood — planks, like the Plank Road, traveling not across space but across time. The planks could carry us back to Old Virginia only in imagination, a vehicle for unverifiable destinations. The whole tour, in fact, was a trip for the imagination, despite all the facts stated by the guides. How can we be among the battle again? Once we understand it, do we lose any possible experience of it?

This battle is one of the most confusing of the Civil War. The men themselves could not see what was going on a hundred feet away, troops drifted in wrong directions, orders were given presupposing situations that did not exist—so reports on Wilderness fighting are especially unreliable, in conflict with one another, vague; and memoirs reflect the directionless maze of seemingly uniform thickets. "We have no definite knowledge concerning the plan, formation, and development of this operation," writes one authority about an important phase of the battle.[10] Another troop movement is "one of the many perplexing phases of our knowledge," we read.[11] Elsewhere, we are told of a "gap of an hour and a half in the correspondence . . . [which] precludes serious speculation."[12] Indeed, says the psalmist, "who can understand his errors?"

The Lacy House was used as a headquarters by the U.S. 5th Corps commander, Gouverneur Warren. You can walk into the large room on the main floor where this otherwise able general falsified some of his report. Of course he had been put into a false position, having been ordered to attack an enemy whose location and strength he did not know, with troops who had not yet arrived on the field, and was blamed for failing to do what could not be done.

Upstairs, the father of Warren's enemy had written his own reports. Yes, in 1809, Light Horse Harry Lee had been upstairs writing his memoirs. He had been in and out of debtor's prison a few miles away. Perhaps here, sheltered by a hospitable friend, he could write enough to get himself back on his feet. We went upstairs to the room. It is a plain, bluish bedroom. You try to imagine a man writing—a desperate, indomitable man. People have reported light flashes, perhaps ghosts, on this upper floor. Light Horse Harry's son certainly lived with his father's ghost—an irresponsible hero, always spending and always in debt. He was also separated nearly always from his family. A mile away, in 1864, his son battled desperately to approach that mansion, to throw the Yankees out of his father's house—held back by the Union his father had helped to create. The Marquis de Lafayette had been a guest in this house, where now we crept from room to room in designer jeans and hi-tech jackets.

It would be nice to think that airy tracings of Light Horse Harry and Lafayette will always be available in that house, and those of the Indian-faced Warren and his staff, along with the tender shufflings of our feet and searchings of our minds—as if the house were some kind of living thing, with a memory of its own. Whatever record it retains, we are primitives who can only read the ragged material walls of it, touch at most a ruddy brick here and there, and walk through.

Outside, the rain had let up a little. We squeeged and slipped toward the house's cemetery, which contains a curiosity. Stonewall Jackson's arm is buried there. A relic like a chip from the True Cross, grisly and, to some, maybe a little comic — but very strange — perhaps the grave of the Confederacy, perhaps a decomposing token of the ways of God toward men, perhaps only another mass of corporeality to which yet another man had to say farewell. That, too, is a duty, and Jackson, a paragon of duty, considered his injuries good fortune, for everything is the hand of God. So that clutching bone in the grave is the left arm of God, having drawn with its sword enough to repay all the blood it had drawn with the lash. If so, that grave on this demesne is the essence of wilderness: the left hand of God, palpable and horrible and inexplicable, and, withal, God's own.

It was a dark noon, but back at the house we saw no light flashes from the second floor. Perhaps the ghosts were on the lawns and in the mansion's fields. Here the remnants of Brig. Gen. James Wadsworth's great division returned, twice, confused and shattered by the Wilderness itself, the splendid general with a bullet in his head now — a man as rich as any owner of Lacy House. The general had volunteered, and gave his salary to his country, then his life. And he died because he lost his temper. Riding to the head of a regiment whose colonel had concluded it was suicidal to attack, Wadsworth shouted: "If you are afraid to lead them, Colonel, I will lead them myself." He pulled his Revolutionary War sword and leaped his horse over the breastworks. "That man is out of his mind," the colonel said, and followed. Wadsworth was also killed because his horse bolted into the Confederate line just as the Rebels unloosed a heavy volley. His division came back here, where it had started on the first morning — what was left of it: not much as military organizations go. On a map in a book on the Wilderness showing positions of the Union divisions at the end of day two, only Wadsworth's is not indicated. Below the map a note tells us, "The broken units of Wadsworth's division . . . have been omitted from this map."[13] Most of the men were somewhere in the Wilderness.

We went back up the road to Saunders's Field, retracing the march of Wadsworth's and the other divisions in Warren's corps on the morning of the fifth.

One of the brigades under Wadsworth was Brig. Gen. Lysander Cutler's brigade, the former Iron Brigade, which had been slaughtered setting up Lee's army at Gettysburg. That brigade had been the most famous, and the best, in the Union army, or in either army, but in the woods and fields outside Gettysburg the Iron Brigade's 2d Wisconsin Regiment and 24th Michigan had lost nearly 80 percent killed and wounded; the 7th Wisconsin, 19th Indiana, and 6th Wisconsin lost over half of all their men. In the ten months since Gettysburg, the brigade had been refilled to where it had become a different unit: some companies were now made up of 80 percent new recruits, and a whole new regiment had been added, the 7th Indiana. But the Hoosiers were veterans, not recruits. The brigade still wore the distinctive tall black hats, still the regular U.S. Army frock coats, and some good Iron Brigade men remained, with experienced officers. Cutler himself had been colonel of the old 6th Wisconsin.

On the morning of May 5, 1864, this brigade had marched past the big Lacy clearing, down toward Saunders's Field, and shortly after noon as battle flared against Ewell's Confederate corps, Cutler's men went in through the woods bordering the south edge of the field. To their right, a blue line of battle crossed in the open. A Confederate later recalled, "The enemy's ranks were as thick as blackbirds. Their flank was exposed to our brigade and the way we poured lead into them was a sin."[14] Reaching the Confederate side of the field, Yankee regiments to Cutler's right faced what one man called "a red volcano." For a time, the blue and gray lines shot each other point-blank. "What a medley of sounds. The incessant roar of the rifle; the screaming bullets; the forest on fire; men cheering, groaning, yelling, swearing, and praying! All this created an experience in the minds of the survivors that we can never forget."[15] The 140th New York melted in this fire "like snow."[16] Veterans of many battles panicked and tried to run back across the open field as the Federal line there crumbled.

Just to their left, in the dense woods, Cutler's former Iron Brigade went in. The Southerners fired with their customary deliberation — "machinelike regularity" which one Union soldier called "beautiful." Bullets came at the Midwesterners from an invisible enemy with "clockwork regularity . . . grim and severe . . . in its slow, sure movement, and awful in its effect."[17] The Black Hats charged in their old way, smashing against a Southern brigade, routing it, sending it crashing back through the dense brush. The Northerners followed, capturing 289 prisoners and two battle flags, charging still, scattering part of an Alabama brigade, plunging ahead through the underbrush. It was the most successful charge these old Iron Brigade veterans had ever made.

But this was the Wilderness. Cutler's regiments could not see each other. They became separated. In such a blind, headlong, crashing charge, you lose your sense of direction. And the woods had been catching fire. Now dense smoke streamed through the trapping trees. Men coughed and choked; their eyes stung and watered. "Look to the right!" shouted a major in the 6th Wisconsin. They were his last words.

The Wilderness can never be fully described. "Dense thickets carpeted a wasteland of hillocks that were generally arranged in rows like ripples on a washboard. . . . Festering little swamps lay in between." "Low ridges and hollows succeed each other, without a single feature to serve as a landmark, and no one but an experienced woodsman with a compass could keep his bearing and position and preserve his course."[18] The "dense thickets" consisted of "low limbed and scraggy pines, stiff and bristling chinkopins, scrub oaks and hazel," according to a Wisconsin soldier.[19] Nearly all the trees were saplings, "fifteen to thirty feet high and seldom larger than one's arm."[20]

When one describes the Wilderness, it ceases to be a thing in itself. For instance: "It is a region of gloom and the shadow of death," according to a Federal staff officer.[21] Such a description is quite appropriate, because in a certain respect the Wilderness was manmade. The old timber had been cut down to fuel iron furnaces — it had been cut down bald and stumpy, swathed off by early American industry. Human beings, considered as a group and not as relatively innocent individual soldiers, now found themselves in a hell of their own making.

But nature is never spent, a poet has said. The Wilderness was laced with spring foliage, a juvenile shade of delicate, green leafery and budding branches. "Spice-bushes, spring beauties, violets and dogwoods in bloom" filled the forest that, with ever-returning spring, was coming back to life. Its glory shorn, the Wilderness was proving death to be an old lie by rising new again. What was hell for fighting would have been a botanist's paradise. Nature often seems pointedly earnest about creating pretty places to fight.

Wilderness, according to naturalists like John Muir and Henry Thoreau, is a place of renewal, a clean potentiality for the man or woman jaded and mechanized by society and technology. But before the wild world was made safe for romanticism, wilderness had been considered inherently inimical to human life. It was a place of danger, trials, and devils in medieval and Dark Ages literature. In the Old Testament, wilderness was a dry chaos through which only by the

Lord's help could the children of Israel pass — proved and decimated and reborn.

As the Sinai Wilderness was punctuated by oases, so the Chancellorsville Wilderness was ordered — in the human mind — by clearings, a succession of relatively clean, well-lighted places. Left to right in front of the ragged Union line, the Widow Tapp Farm, the Chewning Plateau, Jones's Field, and Saunders's Field ran like a stuttered sentence through the sunless confusion. These, too, were human made. Like human knowledge, these clearings gave a sense of clarity and orientation to those actually located in those holes, but they were isolated, and they were at the mercy of whatever happened in the tangles left and right of them.

In Steere's book on the Wilderness, you come across the thicket itself. Here and there we read, "No one seems to know just what happened," and "for reasons that history will not disclose."[22] In discussing Union general Ambrose Burnside's failure to reach his objective and attack, the author tells us that the reasons for this failure constitute one of the "deepest and most inexplicable" of mysteries concerning the Battle of the Wilderness. Even such famous events as the "Lee to the rear" episode are of doubtful provenance:

> An effort to supplement the dearth of first-hand evidence from regimental histories, memoirs, and impressionistic sketches involves the difficulty of reconciling different accounts of the same incident written years after the event and colored with the personal point of view — the coloration sometimes deepened by trends of postwar controversy. Palmer and Venable, for instance, give different versions.[23]

This is a description of History, which is a wilderness marked by a few clearings. We tend to mistake the clearings for the battle. To some degree, it is necessary to do this so that we are not left with a universal blank. But we are choosing our picture, or we are constructing a picture out of the few images we possess.

The vast, unknown wilderness behind us exerts its influence nevertheless. In the Wilderness battles, the Wilderness was the chief actor. Jackson's flank attack could roll up a weak Federal corps but could not beat the Wilderness. A fighter like Dorsey Pender had to ask Jackson's permission — pointlessly refused — to pull back and reform his brigade. The attack had to stop. The Wilderness became a Civil War Heisenberg Uncertainty Principle: you could not predict both velocity and position for any line of battle. The confusion in the Wilderness even claimed Jackson.

Now, in 1864, the successful attack of Hancock's Union 2d Corps was already petering out when Longstreet struck it on the morning of May 6. Had not the Wilderness slowed and jumbled the Federal line of battle, Longstreet's brigades would not have succeeded. Had Longstreet come up on time, the Wilderness would not have given him success: he would have been overrun — but then the Federal attack would have frayed out anyway.

Longstreet's own flank attack suffered the same dissolution, as did John B. Gordon's two-brigade attack that evening. Any attack was an attack on the Wilderness — either side; it made no difference. And when the Wilderness burned, human beings burned, too. It was human in its vulnerability, deific in its mastery and impartiality. It was no respecter of persons; its judgments were sure and terrible altogether.

The only commander really interested in making the Wilderness work for him had been Hooker. Until his nerve gave out — that is, until his faith in the Wilderness failed — he invited Lee to attack him. And Lee was planning to initiate that very disaster as Hooker pulled out. One year later, Lee showed that he would have attacked Hooker's fortified Wilderness line by attacking Hancock's 2d Corps breastworks — and suffering his last devastating frontal repulse. The Wilderness demands humility; in it, the mighty can be weak and the audacious set to naught.

The Wilderness was manmade, but in the end man was working for the Wilderness. In this context, we may look at the battle as a duel of two human wills, with a lot of men caught between those wills, in the thickets of an inexorable, nonhuman reality.

Back at Saunders's Field on the morning of May 5, the Wilderness set a splendid charge at naught for the first of many times during these two days. Cutler's Brigade had advanced a half-mile — alone. To Cutler's right rear, Saunders's Field had been vacated except for its carpet of still or crawling figures in blue. The fires, which were just beginning there, would leave the field and its humans a blackened waste, men's forms unrecognizable and the sick, awful stench of roasting human flesh hanging in the air. To Cutler's left, Col. Roy Stone's brigade had not moved forward at all. The former Iron Brigade was alone, deep in the woods, the enemy on three sides.

They had run up against the Confederate reserve line — Georgians in George Doles's brigade in front and, depending on which way you were facing, on the flank. In a few minutes, the 6th Wisconsin lost fifty men shot, including the major who first realized where the Rebels were. Then another Georgia brigade, under John B. Gordon — whose very appearance on horseback in battle would "put fight into a whipped chicken" — countercharged, seemingly from all directions. For the first time these Iron Brigade veterans ran, along with the recruits. They were in a house of death, and the back door was swinging closed.

They ran through and around Saunders's Field. Here and there, groups of veterans slowed down, formed together, and walked — while torrents of men from their brigade and others streamed past them. They all headed back to the only place they knew: the Lacy clearing. White-haired Wadsworth was anguished and furious. His best brigade had run, and his other brigades had not even gone into the battle south of Saunders's Field. They had marched into thickets and gotten bogged down in swamps, and had hardly fought at all. These were the men of the former 1st Division of the old 1st Corps, which had given its life at Gettysburg and been absorbed by Warren's 5th Corps. But this division was still a 1st Corps division to James Wadsworth: they would be re-formed, they would be put back in order; and they would go back into battle today.

As we walked along what had been Ewell's Confederate line at the west edge of Saunders's Field, we saw that a two-foot-diameter tree had been wrested from the ground by the hurricane winds. Wrenched by its roots, it now lay flat across Ewell's trench. It had been a good trench, fronted by a high log wall. After repulsing Warren's first attacks, Ewell's men had dug and chopped like Trojans. The old way of fighting was finished. You could maximize your numbers and minimize your casualties by fighting from behind protection. Men at war would now be men at work, too, at least through World War I. This was a wilderness of trees, not shell holes, but the principle took hold here. Farther down the line, on the other side, Hancock's Yankees would build high, solid breastworks, too, and as Warren failed for two days against Ewell's works, so Lee's last desperate assault would wash back bloody from Hancock's logged-up ditch.

Trenches were and are part of the Wilderness. The bus took us back on and slowly we drove along the battlefield road that now follows the mile-long fortified ditch Ewell's men built. There was no road back then. A little farm lane had traced together the string of clearings starting at the Lacy clearing, going through Saunders's and Jones's fields and the Chewning Plateau, continuing to the Widow Tapp's place, and going past it to Parker's Store. But now, any time you drive into the past there is no route other than a modern one.

In a sense, the battle had built this route, but commercial civilization has boxed it in. As you drive along this battlefield road, you see houses and backyards come up to within fifty feet of the blacktop, almost grazing Ewell's trenches. Property rights have cut a broad swath and shaved close. The Wilderness in that direction exists only in the imagination.

Ewell's men had come here on the Orange Turnpike and filed off, left and right, to form their lines of battle and then dig trenches along those lines. (They had brought plenty of help.) About two miles to the south, A. P. Hill's corps was marching on a parallel route, the Orange Plank Road. Intersecting these two roads was a perpendicular, roughly north-south road called Brock Road. It was a close thing as to which side would control the Brock-Plank intersection. A Union general and his staff rode into the empty crossroads and planted a flag, bluffing and holding a few minutes until a Federal brigade trotted across the intersection and formed into line of battle. Hill's Confederates, made cautious by the Union brigade's flags and not being able to see what was *not* there, left some of their dead thirty yards from the crossing.

But soon Winfield Scott Hancock's 2d Corps was in line of battle along the Brock Road, and Hill's outnumbered corps was fighting desperately to stave off destruction. The conflict spread along a crooked, confused half-mile front through the dense Wilderness, smoke and brush making one end of a regimental line invisible to the other. Thousands of men along this line loaded and fired, going through all their ammunition. They were then relieved, resupplied, and ordered forward again. In the twilight of the woods, the continuous roar was higher pitched than usual because it was nearly all rifle fire, but so loud as to be nearly indescribable. A survivor said "the loudest and longest peals of thunder were no more to be compared to it in depth and volume than the rippling of a trout brook to the roaring of Niagra." A Union general said that the noise "approached the sublime."[24]

Men could not distinguish their own weapon's discharges. They knew they had fired only because they felt the rifles kick. As men fell, others would step forward to the front. It seemed that men silently dropped dead; it was not possible to hear the sad thud of a bullet, or a groan, or a body crashing to the ground. "Pretty soon those lines in the rear make breastworks of their dead comrades," and still the overwhelming sound continues, a roaring furnace. Fires now burned "in every sector of the forest":

> Many of the wounded who could not walk burned to death, and their screams could be heard even above the tremendous roar of battle. The strong scent of gunpowder, prominent in any battle, was soon mixed with the sick stench of burning flesh, giving this fight a gruesome characteristic unlike any engagement the army had previously experienced.[25]

Sight and hearing were gone, smell overwhelmed you with horror, and the sense of touch restricted you to the immediate horizon of your own body. The storm came from everywhere and nowhere, because the enemy's line was "almost unseen." Bullets would zip near the soldiers' heads. Now and then a man would give up, terrified. Most of these rushed back from the front line, but some threw up their arms in surrender and ran toward the enemy, shouting at them not to shoot. "There is a feeling of uneasiness in the stoutest heart," wrote one soldier, "in facing danger that one cannot see and know."[26]

To break this stalemate, Wadsworth's division was ordered forward again. The troops were to march in line of battle diagonally from the Lacy clearing through the forest toward Hill's left flank. Bushwhacking, stumbling, crashing, the men in the division groped toward the huge roar to their left front. They were still "shaky" from the morning's catastrophe, breaking through the "growth of bush and vines with the greatest of care," wrote a Pennsylvanian. "The fear of again being surprised permeated the entire force."[27]

The first line consisted of Henry Baxter's and Roy Stone's brigades. Stone was roaring drunk, firing into the air and shouting, despite Wadsworth's emphatic orders for silence. Cutler's brigade, spread wide behind Baxter and Stone, labored forward with no shouting, and James Rice's brigade moved behind them. This formidable block of men, five thousand strong or more, blindly moved toward Hill's battling left. Hill had nothing, or almost nothing, with which to stop them.

About 125 Alabamians formed a thread-thin, diagonal line on Hill's flank. These men were ordered forward in desperation, but the Wilderness was their ally. It was unfortunate for the Union cause that Cutler's brigade was not in the front line, because the old Iron Brigade had taken in some useful new recruits. The 7th Wisconsin, for example, had some Chippewas, whom the regiment used in the Wilderness as skirmishers fanned out ahead of the main line. According to men on both sides, these Native Americans were equal to the best veteran skirmishers in either army — though they had no tolerance for standing out in the open in line of battle to be shot. Enrollment lists from Wisconsin show some French names — these were the Indians, caught now literally between two fires.

But Baxter and Stone went forward blindly, and when rifle fire and the Rebel Yell suddenly opened along their front, the terrors of the early afternoon revived. The unexpectedness of the sudden, tiny assault was intolerable to these men on whom the Wilderness with its unknowns had been having its effect. Thinking themselves confronted by a well-posted enemy battle line, Stone's virtually leaderless brigade broke and crashed to the rear, Baxter's men going with them.

A hundred yards or so behind them, Cutler's men were not moved except by anger. They had run for the first time in battle this morning, and they were not going to run again today. They halted and lowered their bayonets. That these veterans were willing to receive men from their own division upon their bayonets showed that they and their dead and wounded comrades had not been called the Iron Brigade for nothing.

The rout stopped right there, but the sun was going down. It took time to collect Baxter's and Stone's men, sort them out, form companies and regiments again in the thickets, and reconstruct the lines of battle. When it was done, the perpetual twilight of the Wilderness had become night. Wadsworth ordered his brigades to move into a diagonal line stretching toward the Brock Road, Baxter in the middle, Cutler and Rice anchoring each end, Stone's men behind. The next morning, the old Iron Brigade would meet Texans again during one of the most dramatic episodes of the war, but that night the opposing armies lay in tense closeness, picket lines only a hundred feet apart here. Chippewas stared into the smoky blackness, and quiet Southerners stared back.

On the Confederates' right, Hill's brigades lay on their arms, exhausted, knowing they had barely held on. Regiments faced all directions, and except for one brigade whose commander ignored Hill's and Lee's calamitous instructions to rest instead of straighten out and dig, they were in no position to resist another attack. Longstreet's corps was supposed to arrive and relieve them, but Longstreet's column was hours to the west on the Plank Road, and would not arrive before morning. At dawn, Hancock would attack all along his line and Lee, watching in the Widow Tapp's field, would see Hill's disorganized men streaming back, and right behind them the destruction of his army and the Southern Confederacy following like the apocalypse. But that also would be tomorrow, as yet another unknown in the dark Wilderness. Tonight, in front of the old Iron Brigade veterans, a wounded man cries out again and again, "My God, My God, why has thou forsaken me?"[28] He is entering the last wilderness, death. If he is to cross over the river and rest under the shade of the trees, he will first have to burn up.

In the rain and wind, our tour group walked the old farm trace from clearing to clearing. Next to me, a World War II veteran tugged the visor of his cap as far down over his face as he could and slogged through. On his cap was the name of the carrier he had served on. These clearings were like carriers in an ocean of brush. The decks were wet today. The clearing seemed more like targets than oases.

But the string of clearings is like a convoy. The larger the carrier we are on, the less we know of the ocean. Human beings cannot abide chaos, whether it be an ocean, a forest, or a universe, so we reduce what we can. Whatever we can get our minds on, we try to subdue under human thought. Insofar as we do that, some say, we lose our chance to understand reality. As we enlarge the clearings, we enlarge our ignorance. Soon we have added bare field to bare field, and made a desert. One way or another, this battle belonged to the Wilderness: it had no resolution.

On the cleared Chewning Plateau we could see that artillery placed here would have dominated the whole three-mile front. But for many hours, both armies were too busy or too slow to get here. And of course, the dominance was only men over men; the Wilderness would take its fires and its splinters and bury the dead. Grant and Lee moved on, but the wind and rain are still here.

From Chewning we walked to the Widow Tapp Farm. The sun also rises in the dark Wilderness, and on the morning of the sixth Hancock's corps moved forward with a roar. Wadsworth attacked, too, diagonally toward Hancock's objective; and that objective — A. P. Hill's disordered young men — was smashed. Cutler and the other brigades in Wadsworth's command — minus the "injured" Colonel Stone — drove ahead in the old style. They belted Hill's jigsaw pieces aside and churned through the howling Wilderness, now filled with deep Yankee hurrahs. They moved so hard and fast that when juncture was made with Hancock's line at the Plank Road, it was more collision than juncture. This gave the Confederates a little time.

The Army of Northern Virginia's commanding general sat his horse at the west side of the Widow Tapp's Farm, near the house. Hill's fleeing men filled the fields ahead of him and streamed along the road. They were not running like a panic-stricken mob. As one of the men said, "We only want a place to stand." These veterans just needed to be put in order; they were not whipped. But unless Hancock's juggernaut were stopped, there would be no time and no place to stand. Lee's right wing destroyed, the left would be outflanked. Hill's corps had by now melted away in front of him. Lee confronted a third of the Yankee army with a few members of his staff, several cannon, and, if only he had been a chewer, the tobacco juice in his mouth.

We stood looking out over this empty, rainy field, pretty calm, pretty detached. But a man responsible for everything had sat his horse here and looked death in the face, saw the wave come crashing, and was empty of resources to do anything against it. The war was in balance in this field, and it did not look like much of a balance. Generals and staff frequently remarked how cool Grant was, on the knoll across the road from the Lacy House, a half-mile behind the lines; and it was noted that when rumors came of Confederates approaching, and someone suggested that the headquarters be moved back, Grant removed the cigar from his mouth and remarked that it would be better to order up some artillery and defend the present position. But here was Lee in the field of battle itself, watching Yankee skirmishers coming out of the woods at the opposite end of the field a few hundred yards away. "Hearts be stronger, courage be higher, as our strength grows less," the Anglo-Saxon warrior had said a thousand years before.

From the Plank Road to Lee's right, a column of men is unspooling toward him, a line of men jogging up to Lee and past him. "Who are you?" he shouts.

"Texas boys!"

Lee grabs his hat off his head. "Hurrah for Texas!"

Lee starts forward with them. "No!" they shout. "Go back. We won't go until you go back." A sergeant grasps the horse's bridle as Texans shout, "Lee to the rear! Lee to the rear!"

Witnesses to this scene disagree on exactly how it happened, whether the most belligerent man in the army was actually riding forward with the Texas line or not, but there is no dispute as to what Lee's presence inspired his men to do. Those regiments charged as only Texans did, yipping and howling, flags slashing, a ragged line racing across the field.

Cutler's men, who had met these Texans before, were not looking for anything but fleeing Confederates. They halted in surprise at the edge of the woods, took hurried aim, and shot the Texas Brigade to pieces. Half the Southerners went down in a few minutes. The lines stood and fired at each other, and then the red battle flags drew back. After the battle, a crude sign nailed to a tree beside the Plank Road labeled the long burial trenches in Widow Tapp's field, saying merely, "Texas dead."

Then a Georgia brigade formed line of battle and went forward, and its men, too, were shot down by Wadsworth's brigades. But three Alabama regiments moved around Cutler's flank and began pouring in fire.

Longstreet was on the field. He had marched his two divisions beside each other up the Plank Road. When the heads of the columns had reached the Tapp Farm, Joseph Kershaw's division began peeling off to the right, and Charles Field's (formerly Hood's) to the left. Wadsworth's men had not been prepared to meet an oncoming Confederate corps, and the onslaught along both sides of the road stopped Hancock's powerful offensive. Although Cutler's men had repulsed the Texans, they had been surprised and stunned. Now James Longstreet had both his divisions in line and they came forward as the Alabamians fired into the Midwesterners from the right. It was just like yesterday: flanked, and charged by overwhelming numbers. It did not matter if you were brave: flanking fire cut you down whether you were brave or not. Cutler's men ran again. They did not stop until they had crashed through the two miles of Wilderness they had come through the evening before, and were back at the Lacy House. Again, Cutler's veterans were noticed: they stayed together and moved back, after they were out of the fire, at a respectable pace while others ran past them. And they marched off the map. They are not in our books anymore; to the very best of our knowledge, they are dead — or they have marched into a wilderness where we cannot go, yet.

Meanwhile, General Wadsworth, in his rage and humiliation, tried to rally his other troops at the Plank Road and was killed. Confederate privates stood looking down at the prostrate Yankee general, the New York millionaire, a major general in full uniform, convulsing, mumbling, a bullet in his white head. His veterans admired the old general who fought for free, who had made the stand with them at Gettysburg, but this war took generals at a worse rate than it took privates — all alike, rich and poor, young and old, no human differences withstanding the chaos of battle.

Hill's men rapidly reformed and Lee directed them to the left, toward Ewell's corps. Finally, the three Confederate corps were united on a continuous front. It would seem that here, union was not so bad after all. Longstreet now assembled four brigades for a flanking movement around Hancock's line. The Federals had been afraid all along of Longstreet turning their left, and now here it was.

We followed the unfinished railroad cut used to funnel Longstreet's brigades around Hancock's flank. Unfortunately, the cut is now on private property, and a busload of flagellants needs permission to bush-whack there in the slop and rain. But it was worth playing the role of suppliants, if for no better reason than that the narrow, sunken lane in the woods sheltered us from wind and rain just as it had sheltered Longstreet's men from sight. Compared to Jackson's famous flank march nearby a year previously, this was much more convenient. It was short. Compared to Jackson's move, this one had also been much more effi-cient. What Jackson had accomplished with his whole corps of twenty-eight thousand men, Longstreet was going to do with a quarter that number: surprise and shatter the enemy's flank, roll it up like a blanket, and then get disorganized to a standstill by the Wilderness itself. Here the race is not to the swift, nor the battle to the strong, but time and chance happeneth alike to them all.

Longstreet had been a beneficiary of the Wilderness Effect in the morning. Hancock's divisions plus Wadsworth had outnumbered Long-street, but in rolling over Hill and pursuing him, they had become dis-organized, disoriented, and tired. Longstreet's first punches had brought them to their knees. But there would be no knockout. Like Jackson, Longstreet would burst upon them through the woods and send them running; and like Jackson, Longstreet would try desperately to keep up the momentum; but as with Jackson, Longstreet would have the matter taken out of his hands.

We stopped at the place where Longstreet, like Jackson, had been shot by his own men. The two-hearted Wilderness penalizes too much success. When Longstreet and his staff rode out of the woods where Yankees had been, a line of Southerners opened fire. Though Long-street would survive, his wounding in its irony as well as tragedy was instantly compared to Jackson's: both had occurred at the height of brilliant, successful flank attacks in the Wilderness.

Otherwise, however, Jackson and Longstreet were not alike. In one respect — though only one — the man most like Jackson was U. S. Grant. A story is told of a Zen archery master who always defeated his competitors. At one contest, the target was the small eye of a raven, the effigy of the raven itself placed high on a pole. When asked what he saw, the challenger said, "I see a pole in the distance, and high atop it a raven." When asked what he saw, the master said, "I see the eye of a raven." Jackson and Grant saw the eye of the raven.

In a sense, Jackson and Grant did meet; Longstreet presented Jack-son's attack to Grant. But Grant was not fooled by the crumbling of his flank. The 2d Corps brought its left in, got behind log breastworks facing front and flank, and waited. The commander of this outflanked corps was not Howard, but Hancock. Back from a painful groin wound received at Gettysburg, Hancock himself was worth a division. His booming voice and commanding martial bearing gave confidence to his whole corps, and to the commanding general as well. Grant knew Hancock would handle things.

After Longstreet was shot, he tried to tell his officers to keep the attack going so that Hancock would not have a chance to stop behind breastworks. But Lee halted the advance. The attackers had become a mass of tangled regiments. The offensive had run out. The Wilderness had said "No."

Longstreet's attack was the Confederacy's last chance, as it turned out — or it might not have been a chance at all. It might have been an impossibility. But a clear and certain impossibility was what Lee tried once the regiments had been reorganized: a frontal assault on Hancock's works. Again the Wilderness would roar, again men would not hear their own rifles; again the woods would blaze. Thousands would fall again, and a short and useless lodgment would be made in that log redoubt, but we had had it, it was time for dinner. We slogged to the bus in our sopping shoes and left the soldiers to fight it out. For all practical purposes, the battle was over. Lee's charge was desperate and futile and wrong, and if it changed anything, it changed only the Army of Northern Virginia's future ability to assemble enough reserves for a major attack. This would be the last one, although the war would go on until next spring.

Like Jackson's flank attack the year before, Longstreet's had been launched from an improbability. The Confederates knew about the railroad cut because they had made some use of it the year before. One of their generals had even surveyed the cut. But Hancock knew about it too, and, as good a general as he was, he should have sealed it off — or at least watched it. The Wilderness was the Fog of War made palpable. The most unlikely things happened, but even then the Wilderness did not permit human beings to reach human goals. Chancellorsville had been a stalemate that Hooker had interpreted as defeat. Now, the Wilderness was a stalemate, which Grant would interpret as the opening round of a summerlong fight. What you bring to the Wilderness, you take out — if you survive. When Grant moved out after a day of quiet on May 7 because Lee's artillery on the Chewning Plateau made his line untenable, Lee thought the Yankee was retreating again. But Grant decided the terms of the battle. Hearing that Grant had gone forward after the Battle of the Wilderness, Sherman said, "This is the grandest act of his life."[29]

The bus stopped along the road where Grant in his own quiet way had matched Lee's dramatic action at the Tapp Farm. On the night of the seventh, the Northern troops also believed that their general had ordered a retreat. But Hancock's men along the Brock Road were roused by the headquarters cavalcade coming along, telling them to clear the way. Grant was riding south. Now the Army of the Potomac spontaneously cheered its general again, in the dark, shattered, bloody, burned-out Wilderness.

> Soldiers weary and sleepy after their long battle, with stiffened limbs and smarting wounds, now sprang to their feet, forgetful of their pains, and rushed forward to the roadside. Wild cheers echoed through the forest, and glad shouts of triumph rent the air. Men swung their hats, tossed up their arms, and pressed forward to within touch of their chief, clapping their hands, and speaking to him with the familiarity of comrades. Pine-knots and leaves were set on fire, and lighted the scene with their weird, flickering glare.[30]

The general in chief simply wanted it quiet, so the Confederates would not be alerted to their movement. Later, Grant spent the rest of the grandest night of his life sleeping rolled up in a blanket on the ground, in a pigpen.[31]

In fact, the boys in gray did think another attack was coming. It was, but it would be some ways down the road, at Spotsylvania. And the attacks would keep coming: Cold Harbor, Petersburg, the Crater, Five Forks, Sayler's Creek, and there was one in the making at Appomattox. But here, in the Wilderness, Grant decided how it all would be. True, Lee had not lost the Battle of the Wilderness. But just as he had been outnumbered by Grant's men, so had he been outnumbered by alternatives. Lee could lose the battle, draw, or win. The first two alternatives were bad; only the third would do. Against Hooker, those alternatives had been two to one in favor of Lee.

Grant had been defeated, according to some other generals' book. But Lee had to break up Grant's organization and could not. When a staff member had pointed out to Grant after Hancock's flank had been turned on May 6 that the supply trains were in danger of being captured, Grant had replied, "When this army is defeated and when I am driven from this line, it will be when I have so few men left that they will not want any trains."[32]

While the South lost no battles for lack of men or ammunition, they failed to win more than one decisively because they had not had enough troops. Longstreet's flank attack needed two divisions behind it. The attack on Grant's other flank, the evening of the sixth, was not only too late but way too little. Even Lee's suicide assault on Hancock's works might have worked if the lodgment had had two divisions behind it. Grant had put it best: "the enemy have not got army enough."[33] Grant could, and would, keep on attacking until the day Lee's lines finally broke. For the Army of Northern Virginia it was not enough to hold the wolf by the ears: *Either we whip him or he will whip us.*

An army is an organism more than it is a machine; it is a river of life. Cutler's brigade had flowed and changed until it was not the thing it had been before. The Army of the Potomac, too, was different now: it had a different mind, and a largely different body. Though appearing to be the same as it had been, still great in every brigade, the Army of Northern Virginia was running in a shallower bed. At Chancellorsville and the Wilderness, Lee had lost his right arm and his left arm, and he would have to intervene ever more with his corps commanders until Longstreet came back. His army had been bled by two indecisive battles. There are no figures for Southern losses at the Wilderness, so writers tend to assume Lee's losses were sustained in proportion to Grant's 17,666 as Lee's army was in proportion to Grant's, meaning that the South lost about eighty-seven hundred. But it is hard to see why the losses should be figured that way. Lee's losses on the Peninsula were higher than the Federals' in both percentage and number; why should they be calculated less than equal here? His inaccurately reported losses at Gettysburg must have exceeded the Federals', so why not here? At any rate, in Grant there was now an enemy who used his superior numbers as no other Union general had before: he fought them all, instead of feeding them down a funnel for Lee to knock off at the narrow end. In the Wilderness, reality set in.

The Wilderness was the last place Lee would be able to collect enough men for a big assault. Here the Army of Northern Virginia's river of life began to run out. But the decision was in a man's mind: Grant could have gone north or south. The Wilderness left it up to him. The intersection where Grant could have turned in either direction is interesting because it is still there. The Wilderness is in our minds.

At the close of the Chancellorsville campaign, a Union officer had written: "It would seem that Hooker has beaten Lee, and that Lee has beaten Hooker. . . . Everything seems to be everywhere, and everybody all over, and there's no getting at any truth." Newspaper reports, he said, were "mainly fictions."[34] As the Wilderness campaign opened, President Lincoln said that Grant had gone to the Wilderness, crawled into a hole, and pulled the hole in after him.[35] Wilderness keeps its secrets. When we think we have it cornered and understood, it moves on. When we cut and pave and develop the last acre of it in Virginia, it will suddenly swell in front of us at sea, or become a comet in the northwest sky, or pull itself down into a hole within the atom. It is bacteria that will kill us by the million; it is the possibilities for the human race and the hopes of individuals; it is past and future: it is most what we are not. Yet the irony of wilderness is that it is also most what we are. We have given it a name that signifies *not human, not us, not me*. But we go there, and fast, in order to find out who we are. We wander there forty years and emerge one nation — *e pluribus unum*.

Each one of us who had gone to the Wilderness was trying to make an appointment with himself or herself. Somehow that is also an appointment with a reality greater than ourselves, certainly greater than the selves we know. We sense that the two realities meet here, and that all reality is one. Give us the rain and the gunfire; give us the mystery we seek in the flesh that we feel. We tire of illusion. We sense that the road to enlightenment is a wilderness road, and if there is to be resurrection, first there must be this tangled life. We will have it abundantly: we must whip it or it will whip us. We will fight it out on this line if it takes all summer.

The Real War

"The real war will never get in the books," Walt Whitman wrote in a book of his own. Why should we accept that statement? What authority did Whitman have to make it? He was a forty-two-year-old poet in 1861; he was not a soldier. Nor was he a politician. Certainly he was not an academically trained historian. With well over 50,000 books on the Civil War having been written since Whitman's time, can't we grant the possibility that the real war might be in there somewhere?

No. Even if there were a million books, all of them written by me, it would not be possible. But although the real war will not be present in what we say here, we can try to understand what kind of war we do have in the books. And, with some help from Walt Whitman, we might even get some idea of what the "real war" was.

Establishing a poet's credentials in History would be an embarrassing task, but in fact the first thing we must get out of our heads is the idea that the real war was or is History. With clearer minds, then, we might be able to see what Walt Whitman was likely to have known about the Civil War. Since Whitman's credibility as a witness is on trial, we might begin with the most qualified attorney and witness of the times: Abraham Lincoln. The president would often encounter the poet on the streets of Washington, Whitman on foot and Lincoln in a carriage or on horseback. The two eventually got to the point of acknowledging each other with a nod or tip of the hat. One day in the White House, the president was looking out a window and saw the workmanlike figure of the bearded poet walking on Pennsylvania Avenue. "Now there is a *man*," Lincoln said with emphasis.

That is the right place to start. Using the language of his day, Abraham Lincoln would accord that specialized term, *man*, only to someone he judged to be honest, clear-minded, solid, and unpretentious — someone the president would trust. Lincoln was a practiced judge of character, and he knew this war. Perhaps when he looked out that window, Lincoln saw something of himself. Both men were poets.

Each of them composed words that go to the center of the war, one brooding through garish days and mysterious dark nights while carrying the greatest responsibility any American had ever borne, and probably knowing more of the facts and historical details of the war than anyone else. The nature of his insight was prophetic — he saw the war in moral terms under the aspect of God. The war was being fought by the United States for freedom and justice; underneath, it was 250 years of blood drawn by the lash being repaid drop for drop by blood drawn with the sword, for "the judgements of the Lord are true and righteous altogether."

Whitman's insight was poetic. He knew what the essential experience of the Civil War was, and he was able to place it in the imagination.

But we should, of course, question Whitman's credentials as an experiencer of the war. Let us compare him to a sound modern authority on the Civil War, historian James M. McPherson. The Pulitzer Prize winner and Princeton professor has worked for many years on the interior Civil War — something Whitman considered to be of the essence in experiencing the "real war." In the preface to his book, *For Cause and Comrades: Why Men Fought in the Civil War*, McPherson explains that he has read over twenty-five thousand letters and diaries from 1,076 soldiers. This is clearly the most thorough job done by a historian according to modern standards of representative sampling. Professor McPherson believes he has acquired from these letters and diaries a basis for understanding soldiers' motives:

> From such writings I have come to know these men better than I know most of my living acquaintances, for in their personal letters written in a time of crisis that might end their lives at any moment they revealed more of their inner selves than we do in our normal everyday lives. These letters and diaries have enabled me to answer many of my ques-

tions about what they fought for, how they coped with the fear and stress of combat, and why Civil War armies could sustain a far higher level of casualties than any other armies in American history and keep on fighting.[1]

Reading thousands of letters written by 1,076 soldiers is an excellent way for a person in our time to learn about Civil War soldiers. But Walt Whitman knew thousands of Civil War soldiers, North and South, personally.

"Nobody can know the men so well as I do, I sometimes think," the poet wrote to his mother on April 28, 1864.[2] In an unsent letter to Ralph Waldo Emerson, Whitman explained:

> I go a great deal into the Hospitals. Washington is full of them — both in town and out around the outskirts. Some of the larger ones are towns in themselves. In small and large, all forty to fifty thousand inmates are ministered to, as I hear. Being sent for by a particular soldier, three weeks since, in the Campbell Hospital, I soon fell to going there and elsewhere to like places daily. The first shudder has long passed over, and I must say I find deep things, unreckoned by current print or speech.[3]

His hospital visiting was not casually interspersed among his work. The hospital visiting *was* his work. What articles and essays he could sell, he wrote at odd times, perhaps a paragraph or two beneath a tree in front of a hospital, and the money helped support his calling.

> I have got in the way after going lightly as it were all through the wards of a hospital, & trying to give a word of cheer, if nothing else, to everyone, then confining my special attentions to the few where the investment seems to tell best, & who want it most — Mother, I have real pride in telling you that I have the consciousness of saving quite a little number of lives by saving them from giving up & being a good deal with them — the men say it is so, & the doctors say it is so — & I will candidly confess I can see it is true, though I say it of myself.[4]

Whitman went nearly every day, often all day, and sometimes stayed with dying or critical soldiers through the night. His letters are filled with references to specific individuals:

> I remain well as usual — the poor fellow I mentioned in one of my letters last week, with diarrhea, that wanted me to ask God's blessing on him, was still living yesterday afternoon, but just living, he is only partially conscious, is all wasted away to nothing, & lies most of the time in half stupor, as they give him brandy copiously — yesterday I was there by him a few minutes, he is very much averse to taking brandy, & there was some trouble in getting him to take it, he is almost totally deaf the last five or

six days — there is no chance for him at all — Quite a particular friend of mine, Oscar Cunningham, an Ohio boy, had his leg amputated yesterday close up by the thigh, it was a pretty tough operation — he was badly wounded just a year ago to-day at Chancellorsville, & has suffered a great deal, lately got erysipelas in his leg & foot — I forgot whether I have mentioned him before or not — he was a very large noble looking young man when I first see him — the doctor thinks he will live & get up, but I consider [it] by no means so certain — he is very much prostrated — [5]

Interestingly, Professor McPherson concludes that the Civil War soldiers did not grow cynical as the war progressed, but remained ideologically committed throughout. The commitment among Northerners transformed toward fighting to abolish slavery, but the underlying idealism and willingness to fight and die for freedom and country, North or South, remained. His conclusion is interesting because until McPherson there had been no general agreement as to this; but Whitman knew it, and wrote it, during the war. The soldiers volunteered for their own ideas and continued fighting all four years with "unquenchable resolution," he wrote.[6] But we did not take his word for it. We will believe a scholar, however, working with only the letters of a tenth as many soldiers more than 130 years later.

That is because we have replaced the real war with other wars. Not that Whitman has not warned us: "No prepared picture, no elaborated poem, no after-narrative could be what the thing itself was."[7] We cannot know the "malignant fever of that war" by the means we are accustomed to employ.[8]

> In the mushy influences of current times, too, the fervid atmosphere and typical events of those years are in danger of being totally forgotten. I have at night watched by the side of a sick man in the hospital, one who could not live many hours. I have seen his eyes flash and burn as he raised himself and recurred to the cruelties on his surrendered brother and mutilation of the corpse afterward. . . .
>
> Such was the war. It was not a quadrille in a ballroom. Its interior history will not only never be written — its practicality, minutiae of dead and passions, will never even be suggested. The actual soldier of 1862–'65, North and South, with all his ways, his incredible dauntlessness, habits, practices, tastes, language, his fierce friendship, his appetite, rankness, his superb strength and animality, lawless gait, and a hundred unnamed lights and shades of same, I say, will never be written — perhaps must not and should not be.[9]

He refers to the war occurring in "lurid interiors" into which his writing can provide only "a few stray glimpses."[10]

Future books will never know the seething hell and the black infernal background of countless minor scenes and interiors (not the official surface courteousness of the generals, not the few great battles) of the Secession War; and it is best they should not. The real war will never get in the books.[11]

Why will it never get in the books? There are several reasons. One is that the "gist" of the war — Whitman's term — was in the *unknown* rank and file.[12] Why in the *unknown*? Because the *known* represents a small, unrepresentative, misleading sample of the war. That is, to know the tactics, generals, ideologies, and economics, is to know only certain *kinds* of things — and the war essentially was not those kinds of things. The war's nature was different from the nature of books, particularly History books.

If we study the Civil War as a subject, or as a thing described, it escapes us. It could be questioned whether the Civil War was an *entity* at all. Perhaps it cannot be known as entities are known. But in modern times, we have decided that in order to know something we must know it as an object. Postmodern thought has discovered what power this kind of knowledge has over its "objects," and how that power distorts or destroys what we "know."

But we can have no power over what Whitman called the real war. The real war had awful power over its people, and still exerts power over us. And we can forget about knowing it like a subject, or grasping it by data, or understanding it by resolving its contradictions, or becoming experts on the war by analyzing parts of it.

We have instead of the real war a literary war, a war only in books — books about books. These books are good and useful in their ways, but we need to remember their limitations. The Civil War was not an event confined to the rational human mind.

Whitman's poems give us some "stray glimpses" of what *kind of thing* the real war was.

A March in the Ranks Hard-Prest, and the Road Unknown

A march in the ranks hard-prest, and the road unknown,
A route through a heavy wood with muffled steps in the darkness,
Our army foil'd with loss severe, and the sullen remnant retreating,
Till after midnight glimmer upon us the lights of a dim-lighted building,
We come to an open space in the woods, and halt by the dim-lighted building,
'Tis a large old church at the crossing roads, now an impromptu hospital,

Entering but for a minute I see a sight beyond all the pictures and
poems ever made,
Shadows of deepest, deepest black, just lit by moving candles and
lamps,
And by one great pitchy torch stationary with wild red flame and clouds
of smoke,
By these, crowds, groups of forms vaguely I see on the floor, some in the
pews laid down,
At my feet more distinctly a soldier, a mere lad, in danger of bleeding to
death, (he is shot in the abdomen,)
I stanch the blood temporarily, (the youngster's face is white as a lily,)
Then before I depart I sweep my eyes o'er the scene fain to absorb it all,
Faces, varieties, postures beyond description, most in obscurity, some of
them dead,
Surgeons operating, attendants holding lights, the smell of ether, the
odor of blood,
The crowd, O the crowd of the bloody forms, the yard outside also fill'd,
Some on the bare ground, some on planks or stretchers, some in the
death-spasm sweating,
An occasional scream or cry, the doctor's shouted orders or calls,
The glisten of the little steel instruments catching the glint of the
torches,
These I resume as I chant, I see again the forms, I smell the odor,
Then hear outside the orders given, *Fall in, my men, fall in;*
But first I bend to the dying lad, his eyes open, a half-smile gives he me,
Then the eyes close, calmly close, and I speed forth to the darkness,
Resuming, marching, ever in darkness marching, on in the ranks,
The unknown road still marching.[13]

The poem considered in its entirety is more like a dream than anything
else. The following excerpt is from "The Wound Dresser":

But in silence, in dreams' projections,
While the world of gain and appearance and mirth goes on,
So soon what is over forgotten, and waves wash the imprints off the
sand,
With hinged knees returning I enter the doors, (while for you up there,
Whoever you are, follow without noise and be of strong heart.)

Bearing the bandages, water and sponge,
Straight and swift to my wounded I go . . .

I dress a wound in the side, deep, deep,
But a day or two more, for see the frame all wasted and sinking,
And the yellow-blue countenance see. . . .

Thus in silence in dreams' projections,
Returning, resuming, I thread my way through the hospitals,
the hurt and wounded I pacify with soothing hand,
I sit by the restless all the dark night . . .[14]

"The Artilleryman's Vision" shows us a veteran long after the war, sleeping beside his wife. A "vision" — actually a waking dream — "presses upon" him:

The engagement opens there and then in fantasy unreal,
The skirmishers begin, they crawl cautiously ahead, I hear the irregular
    snap! snap!
I hear the sounds of the different missiles, the short *t-h-t! t-h-t!* of the
    rifle-balls,
I see the shells exploding leaving small white clouds, I hear the great
    shells shrieking as they pass,
The grape like the hum and whirr of wind through the trees,
    (tumultuous now the contest rages,)
All the scenes at the batteries rise in detail before me again . . .
    . . .
And ever the sound of the cannon far or near, (rousing even in dreams
    a devilish exultation and all the old mad joy in the depths of my
    soul,)
And ever the hastening of infantry shifting positions, batteries, cavalry,
    moving hither and thither,
(The falling, dying, I heed not, the wounded dripping and red I heed
    not, some to the rear are hobbling,)
Grime, heat, rush, aide-de-camps galloping by or on a full run,
With the patter of small arms, the warning *s-s-t* of the rifles, (these in
    my vision I hear or see,)
And bombs bursting in air, and at night the vari-color'd rockets.[15]

Finally, two references to flags in "Song of the Banner at Daybreak" are especially significant:

Banner so broad advancing out of the night . . .
. . . O you banner leading the day with stars brought from the night.[16]

A prose description, perhaps more a catalogue than description, gives another "stray glimpse" of what kind of thing the Civil War was:

Of that many-threaded drama with its sudden and strange surprises, its confounding of prophecies, its moments of despair, the dread of foreign interference, the interminable campaigns, the bloody battles, the mighty and cumbrous and green armies, the drafts and bounties — the immense money expenditure like a heavy-pouring constant rain — with, over the whole land the last three years of the struggle, an unending, universal mourning wail of women, parents, orphans — the marrow of the tragedy concentrated in those army hospitals (it seemed sometimes as if the whole interest of the land, North and South, was one vast central hospital, and all the rest of the affair but flanges) — those forming the untold and unwritten history of the war — infinitely greater (like life's) than the few scraps and distortions that are ever told or written. Think how much, and of importance, will be — how much, civic and military, has already been buried in the grave, in eternal darkness.[17]

The real war was not movements or maps; it was not enlistments and discharges; it was not the relative abilities of officers and politicians. Nor was the real war manufacturing and supply; it was not regimental formations and battery organization, solid shot or shoes for horses; it was not numbers and losses, nor even killed and wounded, or battlefields and cemeteries. It was not anything we can count, measure, or read. The real war was a nightmare.

Only when we begin to think of the Civil War the way we think about a nightmare will we begin to experience the real war. We think about nightmares differently from how we think of academic subjects. Our knowledge of dreams is strange by everyday standards. A nightmare is not a function of the rational mind, though all the props, tools, and trappings of our everyday rational mind might appear in it.

A nightmare has a familiar yet lurid quality; it overpowers our whole thought and feeling with a deep and uncanny force. Writing all its details cannot preserve, much less convey, the strangely whole, intense, and compelling life of that dream. Where it comes from, we do not know, though we can name enough causes at all but the deepest levels: why now, why this — why? From what immense and wily deep did it come? The more irrational and irreducible the dream is, the more lasting and insistent it will remain, and the more terrible. We are fully enlisted in it; we live more seriously in this awful nightmare than we do in our waking lives.

That is why the real war is left for dreaming philosophers and poets to guess at and suffer and suggest. If it exists at all today, the real Civil War exists in imaginations. Whatever connects America's waking dream, its nightmare of the 1860s, and us — that is our means of getting some stray glimpses of that war. The means are song and story, images, strange things, dreamlike things, things to lead us now and then to nightmare.

But the Civil War was not simply a nightmare; it is an *unresolved* nightmare. Nobody has ever figured it out. We keep having it and it never lets all of us rest. We are still Americans and still, sometimes, we are caught in mists and shreds of Civil War America. The elements of this bad dream have not gone away. The black man's moan is still in the wind, the marching of millions for freedom still tramps, tramps, tramps. But more than this, a vast and towering force has spun the American waters down to their darkest depths, and the eddies, ripples, shadows, and slow currents are not yet spent. We cannot explain what happened to us, but the nightmare haunts us still. Even the rational daylight of the twentieth century has been moody at unexpected moments, like a day that follows an appalling nightmare. We are horrified and injured, and we do not know why. Who are we? Where are we? We should be able to understand something from this terrifying dream, but we do not know what. What each lurid image, each strangely alive yet fated dead hero means, we do not know. Meaning is there, but we cannot seem to discover it. Lincoln steps toward us and smiles; we know he is dead, yet he reaches out and hands us something — *what was it?* But it is raining, there is a bandage and runny blood; an army, so it seems, is marching somewhere for a repetitious song is in the air, yet the sound of muffled drums follows behind. Here in sunny Washington everyone is strangely, fiercely, undeterably excited, and a peg-legged soldier in officer's dress raises his brilliant gold and silver sword and shouts, reviles, curses — and here on the silent farm, Sister stands hooded in a black bonnet and we smell the strong, sweet fragrance of lilac.

We awake and do not understand. We pass the day a little distracted, a little subdued, from time to time dropping into abstracted thought. The real war will never get in the books.

"Nothing but Omnipotence"

Orion dominates the night sky in winter. In the clear cold, the stars of this beautiful constellation move slowly westward over the still, dark dome, as they have for thousands of years. The Hindus knew the constellation as a stag; to the ancient Chinese it was the White Tiger. Arabians called it "The Giant." To the Greeks it was a hunter, right arm lifting a club high as his left warded off Taurus, the charging bull.

In that upper right arm is the supergiant star Alpha Orionis, known popularly as Betelgeuse, a star that dwarfs the sun. It would require the orbit of Mars to measure its circumference. It is an old star, burning red-orange in the still sky.

Down at the Hunter's left foot is the constellation's other first magnitude star, Rigel. This blue-white star seems to burn with the same brightness as Betelgeuse, but that is an illusion. Where Betelgeuse burns a phenomenal twelve hundred times as brightly as our sun, Rigel flares a stupendous fifteen thousand times brighter. Betelgeuse is two hundred light years from us; Rigel is five hundred. Were Rigel as close as Betelgeuse, its brightness would challenge the moon's.

At the Hunter's left hand is the blue star Bellatrix; the three stars of the belt are also blue; and at the right foot Saiph, also a blue star, adds to the purity and coldness of winter night. But like Betelgeuse and Rigel, these five are different distances from us. In the belt, Delta Orionis is really a double star; and in the sword hanging from the belt, Theta is a quadruple star. The Great Nebula in the middle of the figure seems to spread its ghostly turquoise, blue, and white cloud out among the stars that outline the figure.

But it does not. It, too, keeps its own unique distance from earth, and shares no space with the stars we see as being within its ethereal cloud. Orion, of course, is not what it seems to be. Ten thousand years ago, it did not look exactly the way it does now, but very close, because of the unimaginable distances within our own galaxy. A million years from now, however, the stars in Orion will have gone farther along their own separate ways; the figure will bend out of its present shape and appear to be another form. Even now, the figure of Orion is only a result of perspective. We seem to look at it head-on, as if the sky were flat. Were we to travel to a different point in space, perhaps to the side of Orion, the design would lose all configuration and we would see the stars to be spread out at vastly removed intervals — here one deeper, there another close by. The figure might appear to be that of a cat leaping, a dim red eye upon us, its glinting claws gleaming through a shower of stars.

The Civil War was and is a powerhouse generator of facts. Like the red star Betelgeuse, the war is a continual explosion of information, most of which reaches us well over a hundred years after it was fired. If all the facts of the Civil War were aligned in single file, they would stretch from Alpha Orionis to within 1.8237 million miles of Rigel.

One of the most interesting things about Civil War facts is that they often change. For example, the bayonet was once an effective Civil War weapon. Then, during the thirty years or so from 1960 to 1990 it was not. Now it is again. It was a wonderful war — from the bookmaker's standpoint. Another good example is the fact that Union soldiers fought to abolish slavery. This became a bogus fact for a long time; that is to say, a virtual, or at least tentative, falsehood. Now, thanks to James M. McPherson's work on why the Federals fought, it is a fact again. This is a rather important fact, despite its checkered career.

A recent book review by David Brion Davis supplies a good introduction to changes in important facts.[1] (The subject at the moment is not merely changing *interpretations*; we all know interpretations change.) Reviewing a book on slave families, Davis takes us through what he terms "historical revisionism and counter-revisionism."[2] For more than a generation one book, Ulrich Bonnell Phillips's *American*

Negro Slavery, fixed a fairly benign picture of slave treatment in the scholarly imagination:

> the reader is told about small slave children playing in plantation "nurs-eries" under the supervision of older children and kindly-looking, elderly Negro women. Nursing mothers come in from the fields three times a day, always resting for a "cooling off" period before feeding their infants.[3]

And blah blah. The slave system, according to Phillips, was character-ized by "a kindly paternalism, combined with a concern for order, disci-pline, good health, and productivity."[4] The period of this book's influ-ence began following World War I, after nearly all the former slaves were dead, unfortunately, because these new facts about their former bondage would have comforted them.

They certainly must have been comforting for many whites. But that was soon to end.

> In 1956 Kenneth M. Stampp, in his revolutionary book *The Peculiar Institution*, demolished Phillips's portrait of benevolent paternalism and described the full horrors of human beings being owned in a laissez-faire society.[5]

This was quite a revelation, the idea that human slavery was an atrocity. Clearly, a profound grasp of the obvious has not been a qualification for Civil War study. One of the results of slavery's horror, wrote Stampp, was the "general instability of slave families," meaning that families were run by women; "most fathers and even some mothers" were "indif-ferent toward their children," and there was "widespread sexual promis-cuity among both men and women."[6] This assessment of slave families was supported by Daniel Patrick Moynihan in 1965. He wrote that "deep-seated distortions in the life of the Negro American" gave rise to a continuing "tangle of pathology" among their descendants.[7]

Not so! charged Herbert G. Gutman, who in 1976 wrote a book to demolish not only Stampp and Moynihan, but also a slew of others.

> Gutman claimed that in all parts of the South, on plantations large and small, most slaves lived in households headed by two parents. . . . And according to this cheerful account, the black family remained strong and vigorous.[8]

So the fact of slave families being "matrifocal" in Moynihan's book was not a true fact, but a false fact, and the truly factual fact was that families were solid.

Not surprisingly, the reviewer tells us that Gutman "overreacted" to the books he was trying to refute. No doubt we can all be sure that the controversy ends here, and there will be no further facts and false-hoods, actions and overreactions, or swings of the scholarly pendulum. Facts are facts.

My point is not that professors, scholars, and Civil War writers are fools. Least of all is it my intention to single out studies of slavery for ridicule, as this field is of the highest significance. We have here merely a visible and current example of the difficulties and limitations of tradi-tional scholarship. The excitement of scholars mashing each other is a refined version of World Wrestling Federation matches, and has its place. As an exercise of the healthy exchange and correction of re-search and ideas, the grunts and slams constitute an edifying spectacle, as long as we discern the quality of illusion in it all and do not mistake facts for truth — or rather do not mistake the nature of historical fact.

The point is that the firmament of facts presents to us constella-tions, first looking like one thing, then another. When you look closely at one of Orion's stars, it turns out to be a binary star — two appearing as one. It took a couple of hundred years for astronomers to realize that the Great Nebula in Orion was not all one: there is a "puff," a second nebula, beside it. The Hunter is virtually awash in the haze of this Great Nebula, or Nebulae, and that is closer to the point. As there was a "fog of war" during the years 1861–65, so there is a fog of history. Today's fog is yesterday's fog magnified, reflected off clouds of dust, distorted by crude lenses, selectively observed, moving with disconcerting speed and never exactly the same twice.

But to cast doubt on the objective reliability of History as a field of human knowledge is not novel, especially today, nor, although it is useful to a point, is such skepticism entirely desirable or even feasible. "What shall we do?" some might ask. "Leave History to the poets and novelists? Shall we drop all pretense and simply agree that History is only and entirely what we make it, and go on to use it for whatever we want?" That is exactly the challenge to History posed by "postmodern" thought.

Sometimes you want to know exactly, or as closely as possible, where your ancestor died. It is the same question as asking where your husband or father fell last week. Here we need those researchers who are not paralyzed by postmodern skepticism. But sometimes we want to know *why* your husband or father was there. Now we must retrieve that intended slur on "poets and novelists." Your father enlisted for the poet's reasons, and under the novelist's circumstances. As if war were more different from poetry and fantasy than from numbers. Astrono-mers measure the magnitudes of stars, and poets name them.

When it comes to the color of stars, perhaps the poet, the astronomer, and the backyard stargazer meet. Maybe such is also the case with that most nebulous and dominate Civil War constellation: Why did they fight? Why is the Hunter up in the sky?

Can the forces in Civil War soldiers' hearts be quantified and shown to us? To find out why Northern soldiers fought, James McPherson read over twenty-five thousand documents — about half the number of stars you can see in the night sky if you are at sea. McPherson points out that the question of what Northern men fought for typically has been "framed only in static terms, rather than dynamic and evolutionary terms." That is, they fought for Union early in the war, but by the fall of 1864 the "overwhelming majority," or about 75 percent, believed that abolishing slavery and preserving the Union were "one goal."[9] Corresponding, but of course different, reasons were found for why Southerners fought. It would be difficult to improve upon or impeach the judgment of this sound and most thorough of Civil War scholars.

But what was the question? It was, Why did they fight the Civil War? Abraham Lincoln asked this question, too, even though he presumably knew Professor McPherson's answer firsthand. And he went on asking the question into the last months of the war. Same words, different question.

Why did they fight the war? Donald Kagan answers a different question, though worded the same:

> In the fifth century B.C., I believe Thucydides provided a clearer, more profound, more elegant, and comprehensive explanation of why people organized in states are moved to fight wars. He . . . understood war as the armed competition for power . . . "by a necessity of their nature [human beings] rule as far as their power permits." And he also explained why they sought it. In the struggle for power . . . people go to war out of "honor, fear, and interest."[10]

Such an answer does not aim at the question, Why did they fight *this* war, as distinct from others? Thucydides and Kagan are generalizing, it is true, but in doing so they mean to answer the question *Why?* as people ask it more deeply. Lincoln knew his soldiers were fighting for Freedom and Union, but *why* did the war come about, and *why* does the war go on? Why did Father die?

McPherson's work supplies still more reason to believe that what you go to war for and what you fight for can be two different things. At the beginning, Yankees fought for Union; at the end, they fought for emancipation. The reason changed, but those at the end *fought,* and those at the beginning *fought* — that much is clear. In many cases, the same soldier fought for a reason that became another, or developed, or was added to. The common denominator is fighting; the surface for the compulsion to fight changed like the surface of a lake. I think the compulsion is primary, and the reasons merely its servants.

You have to step back from the surface reasons if you hope to glimpse the large, deep body of force lying under the soldiers' motivations. One well-known letter might help us to catch this glimpse. Millions of people watching Ken Burns's *The Civil War* heard the letter that follows, written by Sullivan Ballou of the 2d Rhode Island:

> Sarah, my love for you is deathless. It seems to bind me with mighty cables that nothing but omnipotence can break. And yet my love of country comes over me like a strong wind and bears me irresistibly with all those chains to the battlefield.

For that "love of country" he was willing, "perfectly willing," to give up everything, "to lay down all my joys in this life," he wrote. It was the same for Johnny Reb and Billy Yank. It is hard to contrast and judge reasons for fighting when they are the same. Yes, states' rights and emancipation were reasons for each man fighting, but what really *moved* them was love of country. This must have been true of volunteer soldiers in virtually all times and places.

We can discover a myriad of different reasons for fighting a myriad of different wars. But the German on the Russian front, the volunteer Marine in Vietnam, the defender of the pass at Thermopylae, all fought for love of country. "Why did Father die?" Not for freedom or for union, not for states' rights or *Lebensraum*, but for love of country. He enlisted for freedom; he died for love of country.

The energy for purposes achieved in the Civil War was supplied by a generator called Love of Country. But this answer is not yet satisfying. Presumably one can love his or her country in peacetime also. Perhaps we should step back again and try to see what "love of country" is. Psychologists and sociologists could describe the phenomenon, but their explanations would look unsatisfyingly external. There are psychological forces exerted by groups; there is a desire to belong; there is fear; there is even a desire for death, some would say; others would say there is a spirit of the time; and still others would say that mass hysteria generates conformity.

One reason these explanations leave us indifferent is that they do not relate causes to results. The results of Civil War fighting were ultimate: death. "Mass hysteria" does not explain death any more than states' rights does. Love, says the poet of the "Song of Songs" — love is as strong as death. If love of country, for which someone gives up the person he loves most, cannot be explained in terms appropriate to the power of love itself, then there has been no explanation. What is this force that Sullivan Ballou felt sweep over him and carry him, "irresistibly" he says, to the battlefield? What force drives through the fuse he calls "love of country?"

"I claim not to have controlled events," Abraham Lincoln said, "but confess plainly that events have controlled me."[11] Certainly Lincoln stood at the center of the storm. His debates with Stephen Douglas, his entry into the presidential race of 1860, his handling of the Fort Sumter crisis, his Emancipation Proclamation — indeed, his entire conduct of the war — make him, more than anyone else, the mover and shaper of our tragic conflict. However, like many tragic heroes, Lincoln became convinced that a greater force than he was at work.

> The will of God prevails. In great contests each party claims to act in accordance with the will of God. Both *may* be, and one *must* be wrong. God can not be *for*, and *against* the same thing at the same time. In the present civil war it is quite possible that God's purpose is something different from the purpose of either party — and yet human instrumentalities, working just as they do, are of the best adaptation to effect His purpose. I am almost ready to say this is probably true — that God wills this contest, and wills that it shall not end yet. By his mere quiet power, on the minds of the now contestants, He could have either *saved* or *destroyed* the Union without a human contest. Yet the contest began. And having begun He could give the final victory to either side any day. Yet the contest proceeds.[12]

"People make choices" is a common statement today. There is a dead man on the battlefield at Gettysburg, hunched over a pathetic handful of photographs of his young children. Sullivan Ballou dies one week after writing that letter to his wife Sarah. "People make choices." Yes, they do; but then, *do they?*

I claim not to have controlled events, but confess plainly that events have controlled me.

Historians cannot busy themselves with fate. That is the realm of mystics, poets; that is outside the province of History. But the province of History can be variously defined. History knows only what History asks. The more it tries to look like science, the less it asks. The more it denies the validity of other kinds of knowledge, the less it is History, because it deals less and less with human experience. "Johnny, your father died because of the 0.8 probability that he went to war for states' rights. That might not answer your question; however, it is the only respectable answer." But to Johnny, the chief facts of the moment are that his father lived, and was a human being.

Johnny, your father made a choice. History today can tell you what that choice was. Greek poets and philosophers living long ago could tell you something about the nature of his choice.

For years our schools have taught the misconception that a tragic character has a tragic "flaw." But the word Aristotle used in describing the tragedy that Sophocles had put on the stage really means "mistake." The results of the hero's mistake are out of proportion to that mistake; if this were not so, then tragedy would not evoke the pity and fear Aristotle wrote about: pity for the hero, fear for ourselves. When King Oedipus chose to seek an answer to the question of his birth he was blinded and exiled. The Union soldier at Gettysburg enlisted and was subsequently killed. Each person was borne along, as Sullivan Ballou says, "irresistibly," either through the agency of his own personality or through love of country. This force is like a "strong wind" that blows wherever it wills. "The will of God prevails," wrote Abraham Lincoln. We can call it fate. We can call it what we will.

"So Father died because God willed it?" Like Hector and Achilles before the walls of Troy, your father lived and died by the will of the gods. We may rage at them, question them, or challenge them, but we must finally submit to them.

History is too ironic to be our property. Its results are too far-reaching to foresee — and often contrary to what we expect. America fights Germany in World War I to make the world safe for democracy; twenty years later Germany poses the greatest threat yet to democracy; twenty years after that, Germany is America's strongest democratic ally in Europe. The Vietnam War ends in American retreat; twenty years later Americans are selling Coca-Cola in Hanoi. History's causes, effects, even facts, are complex; they change like constellations with time and points of vantage. What has been said in Physics might also be said in History: the universe is not only stranger than we imagine, it is stranger than we *can* imagine. We are moved by forces deeper than we know. The will of God prevails.

Orion rises in the winter sky, existing only in the human mind.

A Soldier's Grave

Walk up a back road behind a farm where I worked one summer, go past the drafty relic of a long-abandoned church, and you find a dozen graves. You can sit, if you like, on a long warm afternoon, if the haying has been done and nothing short-term needs attention. If the word *morbid* comes to mind, then you are too much in the present era and tainted with its giddy evasiveness; the nineteenth-century word might be *contemplative* or *musing* or even *melancholy*. One need not be sad here, or unduly occupied with sitting down upon the ground to tell sad tales of the deaths of kings.

Life is everywhere in this quiet place, far from the modern crowd's ignoble strife. The strife of sparrows occupies one soon after sitting down beneath a lazy maple's spreading branches. The strife of leaves and wind, the distant challenge of a jay, the countersign offered by its rival — the occupations of a thrush along a shambling fence — these discords harmonize when the air is barely cool enough to smell of distant water, when the sky is mostly sunny deep in July on a lost hill in Wisconsin farmland, far from any city.

You seldom see a bluebird any more, but here you will see one on a fencepost if you are quiet long enough. The sight of one — a small, round-headed concentration of the cleanest summer sky — is beautiful in part due to its rarity. That such a thing exists at all, pure and breathing, with wings for the wind and seemingly a will all of its own, is a miracle as palpable as bluebells or chicory. The bird is an anachronism: it should have been eliminated by the late industrial revolution — its smog, its cars and trucks, its factories and chemicals and noise and heavy armaments. But no. You sat down, you waited, you watched and listened, and in its time it came. How sweet and seemly it would be to spend an afternoon in its time, instead of our time of the clock, the car, the computer.

A dozen graves or so — long settled, the headstones small and quaint, most from the 1880s and 1890s. But one of them, a little headstone of white marble, is older and has an iron medallion posted on a rod in front of it. All of them have lain in sun and rain and snow and wind, lain under green and red and yellow leaves a hundred years and more. A century is little to nature, and time is nothing at all to that bright blue concentration of sky.

Just the other day the young man whose name is on that oldest headstone, the one with the medallion that reads "Grand Army of the Republic," said good-bye to his neighbors in that church down by the roadside, and after noon dinner his family drove him in their wagon to the little railway station nineteen miles away. His sister, proud but feeling strange, apprehensive and bereft already — tiptoed up to kiss his cheek, and he let her — just this one time, for he was going off to war. Little brother strutted like a soldier, and shook hands like a man; his mother wept unashamedly, and just as shamelessly loaded his strong arms with a box and basket — a pie, a cake wrapped up in paper, dried fruit, a Bible, lots of underclothing and, of course, a pen and paper set so he could write to them each week and be sure to tell them what he needed. She would send it or Father would get it back East if he had to ride a train and take it there himself. His father stood wordlessly, then finally said quietly, "The train's about to leave, Son."

He watched them from the window of the train, this young man, wishing that Mother would control herself a little. But he understood. After all, he might never see them all again. It wasn't likely to be that way, though it was possible. But he was on a train! For the first time in his life. And all the boys from town and all around were here, laughing and whooping.

In Madison they tried their best to march right from the train, but they did not do it very well. They went into camp, Camp Randall it had been named, and before long Mother's wicker basket was empty. But there was only a small pang about that, because the basket made a nice little card table. Good gray uniforms were distributed, well made of stout wool, and any day there would be real muskets to carry at drill.

There was not much trouble, everything considered, and taking into account all the types of boys that collect for military duty. The first letter to the family went off on time, in fact, a little early. He had not known whether to sign it "Brother," or "Son," or simply with his name — which would have seemed formal and disrespectful at the same time, so he had signed it, "Your Wisconsin Volunteer."

Not long after that, they gave him a blue government uniform. Like all the boys, he was disappointed — you could even say angry. "Government shoddy" was what they called the stuff, a shabby substitute for good Wisconsin-made cloth, manufactured by some shifty contractor somewhere in the East, most likely New York. He was grateful that at least his pants didn't split.

He marched to Bull Run and came through it all right. But his letters home became regular, and stayed regular, after that.

A little later — not long as the swallow flies — he and the boys were issued Regular Army frock coats, dark blue, and the Regular Army Hardee hat, and together with two new Wisconsin regiments and a regiment from down in Indiana they made a brigade.

Time went fast, if you turn the pages dealing with winter quarters and new officers and drill and those clumsy muskets they did get, more or less according to promise. You look at his grave and you wonder: Did they bury him in his clothing from home, after he was shipped back from Washington in the late fall of 1862, or did his family bury him in his faded coat of blue? And you wonder, looking at his grave, if what he was and what he fought for have anything at all to do with why we are interested in him.

The young man in that grave is somebody you cannot know very well by talking about him. In other words, he was authentic. He was a living person, maybe somewhat of an anachronism — real to us only as a photograph is real, of a lower order of being than a human. He was a concentration of something. We can know a person only by talking to that person. If only we could question him!

But he asks the first question. "Why do you watch over my grave?" It's a good thing that summer is long, and the hay is made, and the afternoon is slow, because it is a hard, hard question.

Well, let us take the reins in our hands and get moving. We are interested in you. That war you fought in was the most important event, after the Revolution, in our history. It defined America; it developed our idea of federal, republican government.

After an increasingly uneasy pause you go on. I am interested in the war, you say, because it freed the slaves, made us understand not only liberty but also its responsibilities — that is to say, justice. The Union victory you fought for ensured the survival of the last, best hope of earth. The war preserved the integrity of the United States against a future that would threaten free people everywhere.

It is his silences that get you. An inanimate clod of dust would not make you uncomfortable the way he does. We are beginning to know him.

Clearly he does not believe our fine answer. Did I enlist for those reasons? he asks. Well, you'd have to think that over. Of course, Northern soldiers signed up in order to preserve the Union, or to abolish slavery, or to protect constitutional liberties. But he did not. Oh sure, he might have had those, or some of those, reasons. But he did not sign up for *reasons* any more than you and I are interested in the Civil War for *reasons*.

He is waiting. The question, rephrased, persists: "Why are you interested in me and the war that killed me?" You have just given away all your reasons. Or all the reasons to which you are willing to admit. Then an image of an answer begins to occur to you, like the sight of a fox slipping behind that row of huckleberry bushes at the corner of your eye. There is another answer. And now you realize that telling anything but your truth to a dead man is out of the question. You must not, you cannot, you will not lie to this young man. "I don't want to tell you," you say, shifting your legs as you sit and then angrily standing up. Sparrows, startled, bolt from the branches above you, and the jay you have heard muttering scolds harshly. "I don't want to tell you!"

You already have, he answers, and you know it is true. Might as well say it, put it into words, or *one word*: "Entertainment." It's the truth. It is ignoble, demeaning, dishonorable, unworthy of those who gave their last full measure of devotion — but there it is. We are interested in the war because it is entertaining. It might be a higher form of entertainment, more complex than some others, but it is still entertainment. You are a Civil War nut. Some people are train nuts. Other people collect stamps. There are sports fanatics. Some people study eighteenth-century France, or the American Revolution, or . . . Well, this Civil War interest is ennobling. If one is a reenactor or a scholar or a writer or a game player, the interest is interactive. A good concept, "interactive." The Civil War is fun. A high form of fun, ennobling fun, educational fun, useful fun in terms of America's future, but fun nonetheless. More fun than reading the newspaper or watching television.

Whenever you feel bored, or even whenever you feel low or depressed, you pull out a good Civil War book and sit down and in a few minutes you are contentedly reading about George Custer or Abraham Lincoln or Lee's tactics at Chancellorsville or how some boys got their guts shot away in front of the stone wall on Marye's Heights.

"You're an entertainer." You don't quite have the nerve to say it, but it occurs to you. You feel the feistiness of the rightly accused. "At least as pertains to me, as regards my relationship to you, your function now is to entertain me." You would add, if you dared say any of this at all: "There is no need for you to be offended. I am not saying you died in order to entertain me. You had other reasons then. I am only talking about *now*, and I am only talking about *me*, really. Other people make other uses of you. Some people get money by making games or books, some people make academic careers, some people use you for fame or prestige; you've probably helped a few egotistical gray-haired men procure women. Relative to them, you know what that would make you. But in relation to me, you aren't used that way. For me you are pure, educational, and inspiring entertainment."

You pause, feeling a kind of terror beginning to rumble up inside. Are those clouds, low on the horizon? You hasten to add—or you would, if you dared say any of this to him: "I repeat that you shouldn't take umbrage. I am a contemporary American. The most famous Americans today are entertainers. You're in good company. These people are rich. Millions all over the world worship them. Movie stars, basketball players, etcetera, etcetera." Thank goodness, you feel, you haven't actually said this to him.

But he has heard it all. You cannot keep secrets from the dead. Now he surprises you again.

"Yes, that's right," he says, without reproach in his voice, although perhaps a little bitterness. "That's why I went to war. Call the reasons whatever you will, most of us were immensely entertained by the idea of the war. It was more than fun, higher, more inspiring—as you say. Some of the boys went for sheer dumb fun. But most of us went because all our attention was drawn by the war; nothing would compare to it, we knew. We simply couldn't miss it. And, you know, the survivors never had another experience like it, no matter how long they lived. Many relived the war constantly—the first reenactors. War is the greatest experience of humankind and the greatest entertainment, and we knew it."

You swallow hard and shakily sit back down underneath the tree, staring wide-eyed at the grave. "You mean I'm not guilty?"

"I didn't say that," he answers.

"But," you stammer, "but you're saying that you enlisted for no better reason than I have for studying you?"

Entertainment kills, you expect him to say. But his silence calmly acknowledges the thought, while indicating that that is not the point.

After the Battle of Antietam, a surgeon who attended the wounded and dying—who once might have looked into the wandering gaze of our Wisconsin soldier—wrote that we cannot comprehend this appalling power that sets two armies of men against each other to shoot and maim and kill. What awesome, mysterious force is this, whose effects are so irresistible?

Many people will fight for liberty. There might be gross hypocrisy involved, or palpable irony, but in most times and places young men can be appealed to for the winning or defense of freedom as easily as for the defense of their homes. The volunteers in England, France, and Germany in 1914 might have shown fundamental similarities to the boys of 1861 when it came to reasons for signing up.

But the questions always remain: Why did the war come *now*? Why did *this* young man enlist, and not all those others? Why didn't love of country, love of liberty, love of home, lure of excitement, fear of shame and dishonor move those *other* young men, and what force moved through all those age-old reasons *this* time, in *this* place—and for *what reasons?*

If we could have looked into this young volunteer's eyes the day he enlisted, perhaps we would have seen the light of a strange love. Perhaps something inside which he did not even know answered a call the rest of us cannot hear. Why do the stars come forth, and why does the chicory bloom, unless something or someone calls them into being?

Then he speaks once more, and somehow you understand that this will be almost the last time.

"If you see why you are interested in the war, then you will know why I went to war." Once again there is silence. A long, long silence, a silence of years, as the grave becomes old again, and the stone is weathered, and you are underneath the tree alone. And now you know that while your last answer was true, that wasn't it at all. Both he and you are subjects of the same mystery, the same force.

I knew you, you mumble strangely.

"Yes," you imagine him answering. "And someday we shall see each other face-to-face." You look up. Where did the time go? You should be getting back; it's milking time.

You really don't know *why* you care about the War. You were born with it, you might say. Perhaps you studied the Civil War in school and got hooked. But why you? Why not all the others? A parent took you to a battlefield; you were fascinated. *Why?* Who knows? You felt that you understood a moment ago, but the moment is gone.

Why did he go off to war? Together this time you both could answer, "I don't know."

Others have asked questions in this place.

A young brother, wading the winter snow alone — perhaps he came and cried out, "Why did the Rebels kill my brother?" I understand how he feels, you might think, but he too resists our understanding. No, I mean *why* did the Rebels kill *my* brother?

History is not good enough for him. When we say "perhaps," we have left the so-called hard facts of History as it was practiced in the university during much of the twentieth century. But the young brother did not live in a world made by modern historians. If History is not more concerned with *hard questions* than with *hard facts,* it will remain only entertainment, only self-interest, and only an artificial construct made of shoddy materials. It will not enlighten the present, redeem the past, or humanize the future.

On the other hand, we cannot accept "the end of history" — that is, the idea that History tells us so little about the actual past ("actual past" itself being a nonsense phrase according to some) that we can only face the music of our own sphere. We want to know more about ourselves than that. We must listen to the hard questions.

The young brother wants to know *why*. He is not satisfied knowing that Southerners fought for states' rights, or slavery, or to rectify tariff laws. These reasons do not tell him *why* they shot *his* brother. These reasons are historical forces only in the smallest sense. In a larger sense, history includes all of humanity — what it feels, what it sings, what it thinks and hopes, what it believes and how and whether the human spirit operates in time and space, and what it dreams. We can safely deal only with the small, hard facts. But the young soldier whose brother grieves at his grave did not choose safety, and if we want to understand him and ourselves we must ask *why* he did not choose to be safe.

A mother comes and wonders what her life is worth now, and whether there is any sense to it all, and whether her boy is safe and all right in heaven, and wonders how and why God could have let it happen, and then wonders how she will have the strength to go on for the other children. How can this not be within the realm of History, when she actually was here, in this place, asking these things, at some time in what we call the past?

A sister comes, and asks whether the fighting and killing can be worth it; whether there is any point to it at all, age after age. And the silent father, he seldom comes. But he always looks toward this hill when he mows, or rakes, or calls his cows, or hunts. His questions and his anger and his skepticism are deeper than words. His grief has no escape.

As it turns out, all of us here in this place, gathered at this grave, live in the real Civil War. It is the war that "will never get in the books." It is inexpressible, it is unfinished, and it is of the deepest importance to us all. Who was this young man? What was his name? You may fill in your own.

The young man died in a hospital in Washington City, after lingering a little more than five weeks subsequent to having received a wound at Antietam. Whether any of his family were able to visit him there is doubtful. His father could hardly leave the farm, with the rest of his family to support, and his mother had two children to take care of plus her chores. In any case, it was hard for folks on Wisconsin farms to come up with cash for train tickets and city hotels.

In the years since the young man's death the Iron Brigade went on to heroism and destruction at the great battle of Gettysburg, the North won the war, and the Union was preserved. The country went on to unprecedented expansion, affluence, and squalor — even empire. The nation this young man helped to save went on to make the world temporarily safe for democracy, then fought again to defeat one of the most evil combinations in historical memory. Its popular culture spread around the world, its scientists and doctors invented small wonders, it put a human being on the moon.

As always, the future is in doubt. Will our democratic values tame the savagery of the world, or will America's material weight sink the whole of humankind under a bondage worse than any enforced with the lash? Will the world be choked and poisoned by its own chemicals and fuels, or will humankind's reverence and outrage uneasily deny the power of greed?

Will the honor of the race survive the follies of the modern and postmodern worlds, or will we be sunk into a new dark age? Will everything the young man and his comrades fought for be wasted and denied, and the new millennium become these soldiers' final graves?

Our questions concern the real war that cannot yet get into the books. Who can answer "Why?" until the whole of History is played, and all of time is seen as one moment?

We stand up and move forward to the grave. It is open, the cold earth heaped beside it. The family stands around the space while the minister reads a prayer for the dead. The trees are bare; a few brown oak leaves cling to branches. The father stands looking down — not at the pine coffin — holding his hat in wide, callused hands, salty lines running down his face, thin hair wisping in the cold breeze. Clinging to his arms, his wife and daughter cover their faces with handkerchiefs and gasp their sobs aloud. Beside them but apart, the young brother stands with his Sunday hat on his head and his face is like iron. Any of them would have died for the other. We know it; we feel it; we are one of them. We grieve together. Words are torn into the wind. Mortal flesh, keep silence: the Army of the Lord is passing!

A Soldier's Bones

To John Keats

Call him Adonais, until we learn another name. One hundred thirty-three years after the Battle of Gettysburg, a soldier's bones were found protruding from an embankment after a heavy rain. A glass button, part of a boot heel, a skull, leg and arm bones, teeth, and a few other parts were excavated from a one-foot by two-foot space. The forensic anthropologist who examined the remains reported that the man was twenty to twenty-five years old, five feet eight inches to five feet nine inches tall, probably had spent time on horseback, was right-handed, and that is about all anyone knows. Whether he was Union or Confederate — the thing that mattered most to the soldier immediately preceding his death — is unknown. He had been killed by a bullet in the brain, but later through decomposition and probably the effects of artillery, his body had become so "mangled" (according to the forensic anthropologist) that the remains had been merely "pushed or rolled" into a small pit or crevice in a railroad embankment where men on both sides died in large numbers on July 1, 1863. And there, nearly seven score years, lay one whose name was written in the soil.

1. Indolence

Ripe was the drowsy hour when a visitor tramping through the Railroad Cut saw bones. Heavy rain had shed some reddish soil from the Cut's embankment, and there, a few yards eastward from the granite monument to the Iron Brigade, bones protruded. The stranger turned aside, like Moses at the burning bush, stepped close, and bent down. Were they human bones? He brushed away some clotted soil, probed with his fingers. He searched, he touched.

What sleep did he disturb? What sleep embroidered with what dreams? History knows only bones, but dreams knit bones together, put beating hearts to them, turn brains into minds, call forth the whole globe itself—and when they are disturbed and pinched by fact and reason leave not a rack behind.

What flowing lawn of dreams was pulled aside by that rude and wondering late-twentieth-century hand? For us, it was spring, but for the unknown entity beneath the weedy sod a summer indolence had lasted for seasons, years, into decades; and generations had gone by. Neither battle's pain nor pleasure's wasting wraith had stung since that high summer day in 1863. How flighty time had seemed—how rich the humid soil: the soldier slept through drowsy noons, lay evenings steeped in honeyed indolence, a dream at last, only a dream within the fleeing dreams of others. But oh! the embarrassment of bones.

Now comes a hand to reach deeper than flesh, to stroke within where once only someone intimately loved had stroked the farthest outer surface, reaching his dreams of peace or love then — but now, how deep the reach. No, there is no rest for wickedness or grace: the grave's no longer a refined or private place. We have seized you with our calipers and taken you into our scientific, dry embrace.

This is the knowledge we have gleaned. You were knocked down by a bullet that pierced your skull behind the left ear. You were a white male. Your bones, of which we have 60 to 70 percent, show that you were physically fit—a condition of soldiers on the march. Your right arm bones are stouter than your left, so you must have been right-handed. From the elongation of your hipbone we know that you rode horses. You were twenty to twenty-five years of age — no older, no younger. You were an inch or so taller than the average Civil War soldier. Your bones are very old.

We have asked you other questions, but these, so far, are the only ones you have answered. Is duty truth, and truth duty? What exactly did you die for? May we ask, What did you live for? What was it like to fight and die at Gettysburg? Is good to be preferred to evil? If a man die, shall he live again? What shall we do?

Your shallow rut of a grave is like an urn, but the living are its figures. Year by year we came round again; only this time did we turn our face to you. Only this time did the figures on the surface look within. Why now? Why this time, for the first time? Why did rain make this harvest of you now? Why this visitation, us to you and you to us?

But History knows no "now." On a certain date bones were found. History has no meaning. Mythology, which is history falsified to truth, is only a dream; but meaning is itself a dream. We know nothing of ourselves. We have no acquaintance even of our own bones. Our bodies function, thrive and decline, rising and falling on unseen currents like a mournful cloud of fine gnats — without us. We do not know our bodies, we do not know this celestial ball in green and blue that hurls with all the universe's palpable train at incredible speed — yet on this world like fools we kill each other as boys kill flies or gods slay heroes. For History, we are but such stuff as dreams are made on.

Send us away with our scientific questions. You will give us no more facts. And partaking of your September-summer indolence, we want no more. We will awaken you and call you forth like bundled Lazarus, in our imaginations. We will dream with you.

2. Psyche

What should we imagine? Is it fit and proper to share your dream at all? It would seem a soldier's skill to lack all imagination, to function like a mechanism. Yet in the Civil War you volunteers were in the field because of how you had imagined. You were the men who fired the mechanisms, men against men, dreams versus dreams like Homer's Danaans against the Greeks, realities against realities, until the side that dreamed harder awoke to find it true.

The sad occasion of your war enforces now on us remembrance empty of holiness. You dreamed upon the sea of faith, which now recedes across the oil-smeared, hardening shingles of the world. You imagined a universe full-peopled with a mild divinity, three-personed in its power, love, and justice. Heaven spread like summer over all your family's graves. But your struggle for that worldly heaven failed and oh how fallen, though once how bright, that family now is!

> The blaze, the splendor, and the symmetry
> I cannot see — but darkness, death and darkness.

So wandering, quite out of thought and fainting with surprise — we come upon you lying, bone-naked, in the remains of that high zest, that hopeful glory which wrote your cerebellum on the ground. You are as ancient as the Trojans, so at first you felt no shame. We stared at your most private parts, gaped at the embowered couch of your most intense passion, we counted out your prone bones. We exceeded perversion with sacrilege, because you, more durable than bread and wine, are evidence of your fond taskmaster god — who while his servants blow each other's brains to shreds, only stands and waits, with eternity in either hand.

For him you believed what you believed; and now, though un-believing, we live our daily lives within the edifice of what you thought. But its altar, still stone though it is, stands alone and cold. A choir loiters with old echoes on its lips; priests pace patiently as panthers, the congregation is mere food for thought. Where are the pale-mouthed prophets dreaming? Where are the fresh odes to deity? The closest are your bones. You are this hour's epiphany. You visit us with sad divinity; surely this is the hour of our need! As surely as decomposition of the flesh, the grand old faith creates a story with some meaning in it: surely now is the acceptable time! You are yourself a shrine, and the shrine you are is only in our minds.

Do we worship the Creator of Your Bones as divinity disclosed to us by this astounding *Offenbarung*? Has He chosen this brave moment to declare unto us His glory and His handiwork? Is that what we think as we gag upon the smell in our imagination of your bones? Or is He somewhere in that imaging capacity of our minds, waiting for an altar to be built that He may descend upon it in a fury of transforming fire? The very questions cast the sickly pale of thought over our brows and we avert our eyes from you in shame and disbelief. Your bones kill the clergy that would worship you, and now there rise up new clerics trained to make no vows, sing no orisons, celebrate no transubstan-tiations — trained only to handle your bones. In the ceremony of sci-ence you are drowned and only the elements remain: some crusts, some fishes' ribs, some overturned dry baskets on the ground. Oh, some of us would be your choir, your priests, your pale-mouthed prophets dream-ing — but wonder plods through worship to disbelief, when the mind looks at itself. The wheat is threshed, the vintage trod, the mind wakes but to itself.

Let us build there then three booths — to Love, Ambition, Duty. There, in the mind, the intensity of your life and death shall descend in beauty to illumine and transform — and all the other, outer world can pass and we, like God's spies, can sit them out.

But then the bones again, the bones, the bones. It is as if the only struggle in the world were to break out of the temple of the mind, crash through the cloudy trophies there, and let the warm love in. The bones are facts and History will not let myth turn in upon itself. These bones were broken in suffering — and to that skull a fact broke in and let the warm blood out!

Warm blood. The very phrase is haunted by this soldier's love and anger, his devotion and his eagerness, his fear and brutality. The bones tell us nothing. Dead men tell no tales. We are asking the questions now; the bones have entered our dreams and require of us, "Who do you say I am?" Historical fact has not killed a winged creature; it has reintroduced an unknown entity on the thoughtless table of the battlefield. The soldier is unknown to us, and was unknown to himself. What we thought of as the abstract Civil War Soldier is pierced by this particular, by "*these* honored dead . . . who struggled *here*." Any myth we build is shot through by History, and History is as mindless as stone. The unknown meets the unknown. We exist only in our imaginations.

The soldier cannot be understood: what results from understanding are only abstractions. But can he be *imagined*? If he is made a creature in our brain, will he have ceased to exist at all? Will he be like Psyche, the least and last of all the gods? Or will he be revived, as myth, a dream that shares the truth of his imagination — and be like Psyche, the only one of all Olympus's faded hierarchy to have a real existence, being the universe of all the rest? What he is is what we are, because we exist only in our imaginations.

If we try to reconstruct your identity, you bones, we do it based on what we know. We build a myth from History — History that is distortion, made up of the cruel twins of error and truth. We build a myth from a very few notes caught from a song as vast as universes. All the error that results needs redemption — redemption in a kind of beauty that is truth.

You, Soldier, could have been a Wisconsin man, charging the Railroad Cut on the morning of July 1, 1863, or a New Yorker then or later in the day retreating across its edge. You could have been a Mississippian down in that Cut as the Wisconsin men charged, or perhaps you went down defending your flag from them. You could have been a North Carolinian in the saddle or on foot later in the day in that great Southern advance that swept up to and across Seminary Ridge. If we try to reconstruct you in our imaginations like forensic archeologists piecing your bones together, you converge on yourself from several directions like a particle in contemporary physics — all meeting in that shallow, time-washed grave — meeting only in our imagination.

Only there are you real, individual, *historical*. The facts we know about you are abstractions; there is no life in them. In the impossible possibility of our working brains we invoke you, terrified of all you bring.

We will be your priest, and build a fane in some untrodden region of our mind. There, in that bower of mirrors, we will invoke you — not as a solitary deity of bygone time, but as a triune sufferer of battle. There, in that sanctuary of impassioned wonder, let some rosy agony break through, like

> *a casement ope at night,*
> *To let the warm love in!*

3. Brave Music

This painful day wants to fade, to become a stranger. I press the button and sit back — a small blue light comes on quietly, numbers trace across the small opaque window of the amplifier by file, left to right; inside the CD player an invisible laser beams, and Civil War music plays.

> *Just before the battle, Mother,*
> *I am thinking most of you,*
> *While upon the field we're watching*
> *With the enemy in view.*[1]

A drowsy numbness repels considerations — like some opiate in the mind settling, spreading out into a pool. Today recedes. This is the only drug I have ever known, a sweet hemlock making all but the past illusion, obscured and forgotten. The sound of the Civil War song is a digitally accurate stream of Lethe I step into. The authentic score from 1863 was used for this recording, and period instruments. The old words cluster round with many voices, singing a summer soldier's song to me in full-throated ease.

I open a book and pause. O, for a draft of liquor from 1863, cooled apart from this century's garish sun, steeped in the dead of its own day only, with a bouquet of honor and duty. O, for a beaker full of the Old South, the warmth of the Sewanee River forever still, unflowing, petals gathering upon it like a mound of summer-grassy leisure. I would stain my lips with it; I would taste away all thought for the morrow. Why be in love with what is perishing, or be vexed with times that vanish tomorrow?

> *Hear the "Battle Cry of Freedom,"*
> *How it swells upon the air;*
> *Oh, yes, we'll rally 'round the standard,*
> *Or we'll perish nobly there.*

In the book, the 6th Wisconsin approaches the town of Gettysburg on the morning of July 1. They pass two hills, a peach orchard. An order is given: they walk in column obliquely left off the road that leads into town. They trot across a wide field; they approach a lightly timbered ridge, only a short elevation above the fields. They hear a spattering of cavalry carbines, the *pops* of enemy skirmishers' rifle-muskets. Ahead, the other regiments of the brigade move down into a wide field.

Private William N — trots to keep up, the first man in line next to the Color Guard. The colors, uncased, riffle in heavy air: the national flag, the blue state colors with their motto, *Forward!* He thrills to see them, as his mouth goes dry. Rebels ahead.

The other four regiments form lines of battle one by one; they cross the field. The far right regiment goes into a wood. Smoke and ripping musketry erupt. Next to the wood, more Wisconsin boys go in; then, running, the regiments from Indiana and Michigan. Across six or eight hundred yards, down a slope out of sight, musketry, shouts, smoke.

The 6th waits in column in the field. Falling to the ripening wheat in sweaty rest, Billy N — waits, neck and wrists and hands slick and wet.

> *Comrades brave are round me lying,*
> *Filled with thoughts of home and God;*
> *For well they know that on the morrow*
> *Some will sleep beneath the sod.*

Now the order is given: "*Column forward!*" Billy grips the slippery, heavy musket; they all move. On their right, a large orange brick building stands watching on the ridge they crossed. Over the ridge a battery passes to the rear. Ahead is a road, post-and-rail fences along both sides. Lieutenant Colonel Dawes is riding at the head of the column. He is nearly at the road. He shouts the order — we all hear him: "*File right, march!*" Ahead we see several regiments of Rebels pursuing a running crowd of our boys. We are filing right along the fence, deploying into line of battle.

Farewell, Mother, you may never
Press me to your heart again;
But O, you'll not forget me, Mother,
If I'm numbered with the slain.

Dawes is down, his horse thrashing, but he jumps up. "I'm all right, boys!" I hear him because I'm right alongside the color company. "*Fire by file!*" Dawes orders. "*Fire by file!*" We shoot by turns down the line, two by two. We do them no damage.

We clamber up and over both fences; our boys are falling and I am loading. I find myself in front of the fences, a hundred yards or less from the Rebels. As I look up, ramming the bullet home, I see Dawes turn to Major Pye. "Let's go for them, Major," he shouts.

"We are with you!" is the answer.

Before Dawes even finishes, we are running. "Forward! Guide right! *Charge!*" We are running across the field, colors streaming — Rebels fire; we are close enough to see them standing and reloading — running, yelling; can't hear our shouts — screaming. Dawes is at the embankment, flags next to him. I look down and see Rebels with upturned faces. Dawes shouts to a Reb officer, "Surrender, or we will fire!" The officer hands up his sword but other Rebels bring up their muskets and fire. I see a Rebel flag and jump down into the cut. Three of us lunge toward that flag — Rebel faces cursing —

There in that railroad cut I see men shooting, shouting, clubbing, firing — there, where the Battle of Gettysburg reached one of its decisive moments. In my chair I stare. I cannot see the carpet at my feet, the fading late-afternoon light, the lamp's tomblike cell around me. The bent, edge-curled flowers on the table next to me give off no fragrance, but I hear hushed walking. Outside the open window a low, murmuring haunt of deep summer flies now passes in and out of hearing. I look into the railroad cut, where men now herd together, some running down the cut, some having thrown down their rifles standing still, stunned and angry. There is life, in that space, then — not in the fever of today where worry wearies me, where people fret and are hungry, where things always need to be done today, tomorrow, and tomorrow — where but to stop and think depresses one with all that is passing, or is past, or is to come, and terrifies one with possibilities and dangers: with pain, pain, always the world's pain where people are alone, grieving and dying. Away from this! I would fly if I could, not on mythical wings but wings of History. History does not exist for pain or death; it is as immortal as golden, mythical Byzantium. There are no old men in it; no one dies.

Comforter of emperor and peasant, History is complete. We, aliens from our perfect selves, hear its guns and voices as we stand in this ripening field; how the ancient strains fill the air—here with the perfect past we stand alone: even to die would be good, in the rage and roar on these ringing plains of Gettysburg—to lie beneath its sod, to become sod—here—

William N—lies against the embankment. After the Rebel prisoners are taken out, Billy's friends pull his body up to the lip of the railroad cut. There is a hole behind his left ear; his head and neck and shoulder are covered with blood. They leave him there for now. But later in the day, Rebels would charge over this ground, which would be swept with artillery fire. The body is lying in that field of fire alone.

Alone! The word rouses me like a bell. I look up. The CD player has quietly ceased; the company of singers has passed over hill and dale like marching soldiers, away, away. The old songs are buried in the metal drawer, stiff codes on plastic. I sit straighter, clear my throat. Was it a vision I had, of the fight down in that railroad cut, or was it a daydream? Fled is that music. Do I wake or sleep?

4. *Figure on an Urn*

Soldier, we hear you are a spirit. You have been spied at twilight out of the corner of the eye—a figure still appearing like the figures on the monuments across this green field, a silent orphan of those times and these, a bridegroom ever ready for his urned and buried bride. Cold pastoral historian—comforting the comfortless with unchanging, wordless presence: fringed with all the legends, ripe-leafed, of the Antebellum South or burning-bosomed New England, of "Dixie" or the "Battle Cry of Freedom," you are nevertheless the actual soldier, the fact and the actual item. Yet you are a ghost.

How is it that we know you not? Your uniform is colorless in twilight or at night, your hatless head bereft in apathy or grief or salute or accident of death. You could be a young man of the 55th North Carolina, which, pursued along the Railroad Cut, dropped men as a brown oak drops its faded, veined leaves in fall winds. Or you could be a New Yorker or Pennsylvanian; you might have come across the Railroad Cut in your retreat that morning as the Mississippians and Carolinians pursued you, before the 6th Wisconsin reached the ghost road. Your body and bones were mashed beyond recognition that afternoon— shell or heavy canister through your prone middle, explosions over and in front of those flesh-hung bones. Then, if Confederate, on that sad

evening ditched into a slit of soil by your hurried and repulsed com-
panions; or if Federal, left to fester four days in sun and rain before a
gagging Union squad afforded you the fast respect of covering things up.
Which were you? What officers or files were you among? Which mad
pursuit? Which struggle to escape? What consciousness was loath to
close? What shouts and shooting, what Rebel Yells or hard *huzzahs* —
what frenzied battle, frenetic firing, muskets swung on curses, what wild
ecstasy?

Sounds of battle lift the hearts of men to passionate completion,
but Spirit, your unheard pipes and bugles, your soft, soft rolls of drums
alert the soul. Therefore speak on, your wordless battle cry and declaration culled among our brain's clamor, your marching and campfire songs
of home and God heard by us, not with the sensual ear, but more dearly
caught by our spirits. For though you must fade with day, you cannot
disappear. Always, you are here. Forever twenty-two years old, you
cannot age. Your sunny summer cannot fail; you cannot leave your
songs of love and war. Bold soldier, never, never can you reach that
victory, though winning near that goal — yet, should you grieve? That
hopeful glory cannot fade, though you wear no crown of laurel. That
high exuberance, that mad invulnerability will never cease: the fairest
day of the nation's fairest year will be there, where you are, and never
shall you leave it.

Never will you see the cloying glut of victory or surrender, the years
of tedious peace and fattening old age, the greed of those who feed on
the North's success or the South's abjection — never see the Gilded
Age, the hanging Ku Klux Klan, the plump decrepitude of gasoholic
suburbs, our dirty water, the smudged horizons of our leaden air. Forever
will that world of yours be fair.

But who are you, who were ordered to this seemly sacrifice? Where
did you come from, North or South? What little town was emptied of its
folk when the rolls of war were mustered, and when funerals were
drummed upon its cemetery hill? What pious crowd walked out its
orisons toward what fresh-spaded obsequies, the day your comrades'
boxes came home? For you forever will that empty town be still, its
marble graveyard always fixed in distant pantomime of grief.

You are not like us, though a Spirit of Mortal: you are like the
soldier, ever vigilant, on a marble monument standing there across the
field, or like a figure on a marble urn on some state's memorial, somewhere on this moving field. You do not breathe, but do you grieve? Is
your visibility to us a passion? Who are you? Where are you? All that

you are resides in our imagination. All that we are stares back there. We meet upon the surface of an urn that bears your bones.

Like engravings from your war, you are now immortal—all breathing human passion far removed: the parched mouth and aching forehead far removed. Amid successive woes of decades and centuries, you do not change. What do you say to us in that august silence? You have passed outside our thought, and we outside yours. We are invisible to you. You say nothing to us—only, your presence teases us out of thought until we know life, know death, with knowledge deeper than pale thought. We cannot bring to speech such knowledge deeper than memory. Cold pastoral!

You are immortal. Silent mirror, to see you is to see death. One glance undoes all the world, all abstraction, all illusion. Then the vision vanishes. But for a moment out of time we were not abstractions, and you saw us with the War's eyes.

We have the globed bone of your legendary head, in which your eyes ripened. "Alas," History might say at most to the defeated and destroyed, but it offers neither help nor pardon, and goes its way—but the eyes of war are steady. In your bones the light of battle still holds and gleams, only turned low—from which thighbones and arms it once flashed like the fell of birds of prey. There is nowhere where you do not see us. But the immortal eyes are blank.

Immortality is not life. Life by its own nature changes and ends: life is mortal. Life is death and death is immortality—that is all we know in your gaze, and all we need to know. Like a figure on an urn, your presence only touches its lips to the hand of knowledge. Irritably reaching after fact and reason, we learn that death and life cannot be understood, that immortal art is silent, that bones know what only bones know.

You are better then than we are now. Time has gone on; the leaf has broken from the bough. That moment of utmost intensity is preserved for you—that moment when the highest, fiercest passion broke against the palate of history—when devotion and rage and love all burst willingly; good or evil or both together in the apotheosis of human passion, and in that blinded moment you entirely forgot yourself and now forever are that selfless specter. Yet that moment was in time, as was that passion.

For passion to be so intense that it becomes forever, and time to be so full that it becomes eternal, is impossible. A soldier in that apotheosis must die. A lesser passion and a thinner moment of time must move; and later the veteran looks back and thinks that today, by comparison, he is not alive. "We were soldiers once, and young." The price of forever is death; and the price of eternal youth is stillness — embalmed trees in the poppied fume of a glass-tender night. Therefore, sacrifice, you are come to this high altar, forever unravished bride, forever foster-child, the eternal soldier killed in battle. Those who are happy with the happiest of happiness are forever happy; they wake to no dawn. The happy gods never die: the plain brown nettle and the flutter-hearted sparrow are conscious in their downward aging, and to them the gods are nothing. The dead are piles of equanimity. The living soldier suffers.

You are a twilight shape, a still attitude like a frieze of poses set in granite — like the marble men and horses of the monuments on this warm and ashen battlefield. You are as real as any sculpture here, which seems to breathe and in that seeming jolts us out of thought. Time and eternity — suddenly they are not two; act and thought, not two; past and present — one. What are we? Where are we? Is there no escape? Caught in eternity, we are separated from you only by a battle's bullet. We are the same except for leaden consciousness: alive and dead. To man and woman age upon age, you are a strange friend. You say forever, life is death and death is life — that is all you know on earth, and all you need to know.

5. Melancholy

No, no, you cannot go back; the past is in the eternal past. But more: the past is lethal to the present. One can remember, for memory is a partial attention of the present mind, but to go back is not merely to remember, it is to be, then: to not exist. You must forget the present to relive the past. To go inside one's mournful psyche, where the downy owl keeps silent knowledge of your sorrow's mysteries, is to meet that old soldier where everything and nothing press through each other like two ragged lines of battle — and the two cruel deities, Truth and Error, sway the teeming tides with fickle wisdom. Nothing is there but you alone: you are the only population of the past. One could die there. But no, no: the shades of imagination that we are need no nightshade of forgetfulness. Better to die into life, if one wants the melancholy of human life and death and love — for melancholy is the wakeful anguish of the soul; mistake her not for sleep, whose loving kindness seems better than life.

Yet who is such prey to forgetfulness as not to take one last longing, lingering look behind? Perhaps those bones belong to a lieutenant from

North Carolina who went forward with the great assault that Wednesday afternoon.

The field had lain fallow since midmorning. The dead and wounded in the Railroad Cut, if uniformed in blue, were carried out or left with paper scraps pinned to them indicating who they were, which regiment was theirs, which state.

Battery B, the Iron Brigade's battery, rolls up: six brass cannons and their limbers, crews, and horses. They drop the pieces' trails, three shining golden guns on each side of the Railroad Cut. The 6th Wisconsin takes position behind them, while the other regiments of the brigade remain south of the road, forward several hundred yards in the woods and fields. Here astride the Railroad Cut and looking down the scattered line of gray-dressed bodies on its rough floor, Battery B prepares to stand and wait.

They cannot see who comes, or how close they are. Across the hump of hill that makes the Railroad Cut, across the fields and ridge a mile west of the serious and fidgeting battery, an entire new division of Lee's army is leaving column in the road, filing right and left, thousands of ragged veterans in calm and assured rage deploy in three wide lines of battle. Their discipline is adequate and confident. Company after company, regiment after regiment, they bend and flow from the forward-walking column until two brigades stand ready south of the road and another with untied flags waits in the heat astride the road. Its left regiment is anchored at the railroad cut. This third brigade awaits the order to go forward.

"Forward" lettered on its blue flag straight ahead a mile, the 6th Wisconsin, now some two hundred men, resides beneath the same hot sun, reflected in blinding beauty from the six good guns whose mounted officers just now turn in their saddles. *They are coming, now.* The crews move: six men load shells into their guns and step away.

A young lieutenant who began two years before as a corporal walks forward behind his company of North Carolinians. He has relayed the order to move, this father of four. Only last evening he has sent a letter home. *Give them all a hug. Kiss our baby for me, Darling Wife; keep some for yourself.* His sword is drawn, reflects a dodging sun; he speaks now and then: *Keep pace, men, no slowing down. Soon as we clear that ridge top yonder, their guns will open on us for all they're worth. We'll take those guns.* The men in butternut and gray on both sides of the road are marching in a waved but steady line that seems a mile from end to end. Their red, star-crossed battle flags are carried several paces ahead of each regiment's front rank. The young lieutenant sees the sturdy line; his heart rises, fills within him. Now they top the ridge. Ahead of them across the fields is a scattering of wood lots, and to the right an orange brick building with a cupola, some houses, and one thin line of blue, and batteries placed close together. Ahead, down the distance aimed by an unfinished railroad, six puffs of smoke from another battery. In slow seconds as the Carolinians come down the ridge's gentle slope, the lieutenant and his men hear the thuds of those guns as overhead and in the field before them, five bursts flash in red and yellow.

They walk straight through the settling earth and dust. They tread the level field now. Another series of white puffs ahead, the impacts of the cannon sounds match the tearing flashes. Iron screams among them, taking down a man some paces to the lieutenant's left. The lines move on; the men begin to shout. Curses, taunts, high yells; the color-bearers wave their flags back and forth defiantly, slash them forward. Another cannon volley comes, then another; the blue sky with its clouds sails past, the hot sun bears down in ecstasy — forward, forward, now across a litter of canteens and empty cartridge boxes, two men lying, rifles scattered here and there. And now more evidence of fighting earlier: knapsacks, caps, more rifles, haversacks, blankets. We are in among it now — we are in the battle — six hard cracks ahead and smoke and fire. Now a regiment of infantry in blue is swathed in smoke ahead of us. *"Raise the Yell, boys! Raise the Yell!"* Now our scattered yips ripen into one high stream, rolling forward up to heaven, bullets hissing everywhere — dashing with the company's line of battle, pressing ahead of them: the towering sky, the lifting sun, the men's faces straining, eager, joyous, crazy, enraged — bright-eyed — sword lifted — turning to shout at them, *"Come on, men! Give them Carolina hell! Forward! For — "*

An exploding blow to the head. The line passes on. Now blasts of canister, storms of canister again and again raking the ground. The line attacks again and canister plows the fatal air, the ground, the fallen bodies. A photograph in a breast pocket tears away —

No, no — it does no good to die in this imagining. We shall dream and think condemnation upon ourselves, failing to discern the body. These bones are not a living man somewhere in our imagination. They are the corpse of a man. Here he lies, in our soil, in our sight, and here and now in our own day and age.

We must not grieve for that imaginary man. Sorrow and elation are alike unreal; to enter the imagination thus is death, not life. It is an-other country from whose bourne no one returns — but here and now we have unimaginary language. He marched in beauty, this soldier — beauty that must die. That is all we know of him.

But if we wish to live that high pain of life, if sudden sorrow looking into time and change falls like a weeping cloud from a ripe sky, then glut its lushness on the rainbow's thin wonder, or the failing fragrance of a rose; or best of all, look in the eyes of one you love but see them not — see only beauty, if your craving to be drowned in beauty still yawns wide — for of all beauty, that we love pains most.

Such beauty must die. The joy in one we love is always touching a hand to its lips bidding adieu; the pleasure in such company cuts deeply, for in that fine awakening of love, one sees that all such time and company must perish. Or else the pleasure and the joy were mere forgetfulness, a shade held over drowsy eyes, a poisoned, heady, stuporing draft of woody wine — failure to discern the body, the body that must die, the body that changes now in this time, that fades in length even as the rosy bloom blushes. For the highest delight is distinguished from all lesser joys only in this, that in the glory of her brilliant sanctuary, veiled Melancholy keeps her crystal throne. She is not seen except by those who glimpse her through the highest joy: in that vision the soul awakes to consciousness, shares the glory of the holiest of holies, and, divided from itself now, feels the utmost depth of divine suffering. Here we taste the body and the blood of what is given, taste the sadness of the holy might. For holiness is beauty, beauty lives, and in its wakeful anguish only is the soul alive to its making. This life is the image of God; it is everlasting life.

One who sees the dead man's bones tells no more tales. The poet and the soldier is one whose strenuous tongue bursts the grape of ecstasy, and becomes a poetry that he himself shall read. To see pure Beauty is to be among its cloudy trophies hung, to become only vision; to see what is passing is to pass; it is at last to know the pain of creation and creator, and to fall.

6. Autumn

The bones have told us what we know is so, that here in the Cut they struck: the first troops of the Union — the Iron Brigade — and the lead, the head, of the Army of Northern Virginia. Time was all. Time was everything the Southerners needed; time was all the Northerners would die for. If the South could take Seminary Ridge, pass through the part-empty town and grasp the heights to the east, the battle would be theirs. They would hold the heights and the Army of the Potomac would not prevail against them. They would defeat the Union army, march to Washington and capture it, force from the Union government and its wearied people — stunned and stupefied by sacrifice and failure, forgetting everything but grief — force from a reluctant Lincoln the recognition for which they had fought. The Confederate States of America would flash into consciousness and exist down through this day.

If the Union men could hold those west-of-town heights until more of their army arrived to take position on the crucial eminence of Cemetery Hill, then all that day and all the next, and next, it would be death for Southerners attacking that high ground. Victory would ripen with the letting of blood. Exhausted, short of ammunition, Lee's army would have to find its way back south — through the rain, past the miles of wagon-carted wounded, past the drooping horses' heads shedding sweat and water. The Union would be preserved; the armies would move on. A heartened North would listen to the president in that autumn-barren cemetery and believe. State by state and home by home, the Confederacy would be exhausted and beaten. Man by man, general by general, enough would die, enough go hungry — and their capital would be abandoned.

All this there and then in that Railroad Cut, back in midsummer. All that possibility met together with the past that brought them there — the orders, errors, resolutions, the Declaration of Independence, the Dred Scott case and *Uncle Tom's Cabin* and the treaty that ended the Mexican War, and nullification and states' rights and popular sovereignty and the U.S. Constitution, a vast orchard of historical paper all coming to fruition here. All this weighed upon their bones; all those words, and these bones are the time's perfected poem.

Then men marched, raged, struggled, and died. The flower of that legendary Union brigade, brought to full bloom by almost a year of fighting: Brawner's Farm, Turner's Gap, Antietam, Fitzhugh Crossing — now veterans who had seen the worst but still were young and tough — for here they were perfect. They attacked, they captured hundreds — even the first general Lee would so lose on the field — and then they would hold. Through the morning, as the sun rose high, into noon, then through the tense and weary early afternoon. More, and still more, they killed and died and held. When the grand Confederate assault came in midafternoon, these soldiers in blue blunted the first wave, they held on fast, they stood like iron. Longer, still longer, until it was too late for the Confederacy, until the day of victory for Lee's army had passed from possibility to regret; still they held, and held on still — the full perfection of discipline and courage, the last full, and pressed-down overflowing full, measure of devotion.

The Southerners came to fight, too. The crest of their power burst at this apex of their great invasion. Yelling, they went in and took their losses in the morning. Determined men, they reformed and waited while more veterans came forward with the steady amplitude of an army that will be as great here as it could become. These regiments, these brigades and batteries, these officers, had fought the bitter springtime of the war. They had cheered and marched, sore-footed and ragged, across the river into Maryland in the sunny time of the Confederacy's youth, held on grim and jubilant at Fredericksburg, teemed in brilliant concert that early summer day at Chancellorsville — attacking through the woods in fire and darkness as the season grew to this: here they came, victorious, well-equipped, as numerous as leaves on summer boughs. In mile-wide lines they advanced that afternoon of July 1, 1863, beautiful and terrible — among the best who ever were or would be, man for man, in any army anywhere. Here they crested, here the work of Southern Independence reached the full. Here they broke across the iron barrier and flowed, too late, into the town that forever bears inscriptions of their blood.

It would all be given here — all that mattered. The Army of Northern Virginia lost more than twenty-five thousand men. The next year, in the Wilderness, they failed in each flank attack and breakthrough because they did not have army enough. The power to strike was gone. Here, at Gettysburg, it had gushed forward and out as in these men the Lost Cause ripened to the core — and in trenches, pits, and graves. They loaded every rift with brave men — more, and still more, through McPherson's Woods, across Seminary Ridge, up the sides of Cemetery Hill, through peach orchard and wheat field, up the stony sides of Little Round Top, through the house-high rocks of the Devil's Den, up the thick-treed slopes of Culp's Hill like cluster-crowded vines, and finally, the bending, swelling lines of sweet Virginia, fruitful Carolina, gentle Tennessee walked across the fields toward Cemetery Ridge as if clammy summer days and Rebel Yells would never cease.

The Iron Brigade fought its last battle here. After July 1 at Gettysburg it would exist as the old brigade only on paper, passing into History. This brigade lost more men than any other in the Army of the Potomac during the war. Two-thirds of those who came to Gettysburg were shot. Two regiments lost nearly four of every five men.

In the hours after the men fell, History walked here and there

among the rows. At first, survivors made little more than slips of paper with names, or slats of wood with penciled information sticking up
from heads of shallow graves. Then more would come, lists be written
down, letters sent, reports made out and copied. Memories would flow
across pages; arguments would form in steady lines. All had ripened into
words. For those men who tramped across the summer fields — for you,
Soldier — that ripeness was all.

Where are your patriotic songs of the war's springtime? Aye, where
are they? Only the little rubbing sounds, the minuscule scrapings of
archaeologists' probes are heard here now. Today the stubble fields on
both sides of the Railroad Cut are roped off. A square of peeled-back sod
lies open to the little tools of careful, spectacled historians. The little
swish of sifting, almost imperceptible, issues from the fingers of the
team. Their low murmurings rise and fall on the uncertain autumn
breeze.

Recording every particle — a glass button, a rectangular fragment of
bone shorter than a knuckle — the archaeologists number them and tag
them, as surgeons used to tag and number veins and arteries during
amputations on slippery tables through those agony-wrought midnights
of the war. They pack each sifted jot and tittle into plastic bags and
boxes. They themselves work square foot by square foot so that not an
iota in the soil remains unwinnowed. Deep cubic feet of soil and clay
and stone are sorted, felt, examined, rejected, gleaned. Patiently, hour
by hour, the oozings of this dust pass, screened by the steady stare of
History close-focused.

The authorities had let the summer pass without revealing where
the bones lay unexamined. Then, when the tourist flow had slackened
to tricklings, from universities and colleges, from agencies of the government, men and women gathered here with screens and magnifying
glasses, with electronic detectors and infrared photography. The trip of
shutters now and then clicks like insects over the brown October fields.
A pop can shrieks its puny steam. Wispy hair flutters; pages of the
written record twitter in the wind. Everything of this that is to be turns
into History.

We are History. You are what we glean and put together when we
gather in this alien field where lilies wither, this field turning somewhere in the universe, this empty field. With long arms and pale fingers we reach, we stroke, we pluck, we raise a leg bone whole. You are
gone. But O, the brave music! Was that not you? Were you born for
this? You were no Muse's pampered boy; no Grace granted you parole.
Spat blood, crumpled coughs. You always made an awkward bow.

Face-to-Face

A photograph in the Carlisle Barracks archives reminds me that we have taken the war out of the people who fought and suffered it, and put it into books, arguments, reenactments, and movies. We have looked away from those people and made their war into something we can use — seldom to the purposes for which most of them struggled. Their war now looks like a "martial competition"[1] instead of a conflict of causes that moved people's minds and hearts to the point that they would kill and die rather than give up their ideas or muzzle their feelings. They joined the army, and sent their sons, for inflammatory causes like liberty and racism and honor and patriotism. To them the war ceased to be an adventure and became a disaster, a personal tragedy, and a national nightmare. The country's grief is not assuaged yet. Nor have all the causes been resolved.

Those people will haunt us until we see them for who they are. At present, they are merely reflections of ourselves. However, this is not all bad, because we need to have a good look at ourselves. But ultimately we want to know those people face-to-face. For that to happen, the phantom whose image comes between us must be dispelled — the phantom made up of myth and fact that is neither us nor them. Good luck.

Figure 1

Who were those people in the 1860s photograph, in relation to each other? One notices that the faces of two of them are not clear — the man and woman of similar age as it appears, to our left of the group. Notice that a small boy kneels at the edge of the brick walk to their right as they face us. They are his parents. They are closest to him, and they are unable to pose for the picture without moving. Even a slight shift of their attention in his direction registers on the plate. Has the boy just dropped something or cut himself? Is he crying, or speaking? Are they trying to keep him still? Is he about to bolt? Is he about to inhale varioloid or scarlet fever?

The girl sitting on the porch is ill: she has a scarf wrapped about her head and wears a shawl. She is seated next to the man wearing a hat, but appears not to be his wife. She has an expression of gentleness and patience, and she is dark around the eyes. She might have tuberculosis. Her father sits beside her with the quiet, outwardly stable, and peaceful yet protective expression of a man seated next to his daughter for a photograph. The two bear a facial resemblance.

His wife, her mother, stands behind the woman with a hand on the rail. She is really the stable one; she has been strong through the daughter's illness. Perhaps there are other children, or were. She is firm but not scathing; she is secure about what is right and wrong—to be so is one of her duties.

The woman in front is the focal point of the tableau. She is either the photographer's wife, or the wife of an officer away with the army. She can be a little sharp, a little critical. Perhaps she is a bit dry about her husband fooling with that expensive new contraption, even though he makes their living with it. Or she is impatient with being photographed as a celebrity; that is, the wife of a celebrity. She is the sister of the seated man: she has his mouth, nose, and somewhat his expression.

But her mouth resembles that of the girl, too. Perhaps the man holding his hat and this woman in front are husband and wife, and the woman with the light dress is their servant, the child's nanny. The man at the steps has the attitude of a man of some business, habitually adopting the pose of one about to see to some necessary affair.

The woman in the light dress is clutching a handkerchief—or is she? Has she come out at the bidding of the family, still holding her dust cloth? A magnifying glass reveals something odd about the shape of her hand. She has something white on parts of both hands. Her hair is not done in the formal fashion of the two women in dark dresses. Her skin appears to be darker than all the others except the seated man. (This is probably not a Southern family; the photograph is from the collection of the Massachusetts Commandery of the Military Order of the Loyal Legion of the United States.)[2] The dress she wears is not formal, like the ones the two standing women are wearing. Perhaps the other two women are wives, married to each of the men, and they wear colors appropriate to their age and status. The mother stands at the rear; the other three are sisters. The man on the steps is the son-in-law.

Look again at the woman in back. Is that a mourning band on her arm, or is it decorative work like that on the front woman's sleeves? The men are dressed in dark clothing—anything else would be egregious— so one cannot easily see whether there is anything on their left sleeves, but nothing is perceptible. The young woman in the light dress is the only one who might be smiling. Or is the ailing girl also smiling, just a little? She touches the heart.

The woman in the light dress is the only one in shadow. Her face is blurred, not merely obscured by shade, unlike the man on the steps, squinting in the half-sunlight. Her face does not look quite right. Is it because she has moved? Who is she? I have stared at her so long that I am convinced that I recognize her.

These seven remain together although a war is being fought, and at least one of them may be contagiously ill. Human beings love under the hard conditions of their own nature. What holds the people in the photograph together and what gives them life is what also binds us to them. If we can know them in any satisfying way, it is by the same bond; any other way of knowing is mere play with the things in our own minds. Our knowledge of the past, present, and future is the knowledge of a child playing by himself, deep in the objects between his own small hands. "For we know in part, and we prophecy in part. . . . For now we see through a mirror, darkly; but then face to face: now I know in part; but then shall I know even as also I am known."[3]

Look at them. To look closely at that family on the veranda is to see them feelingly. When we look at them, we see that the war was no mere "martial competition."

But their faces are still mirrors. Faces can lie. We are deceived by salespersons, by movie actors. We are fooled even by our friends and family. We can look at these faces and think we know what kind of people they were, yet be completely wrong. If we examine photographs of little-known Civil War officers, we could try to determine which were the good ones, which were the honest ones, which were the well-liked ones or backstabbers, which were the drunks, the father figures, the politicians, but we would not know. We would as likely be wrong as right. We can only guess, flattering ourselves while we imagine. What is in our own minds comes forth. We look again at the photograph of those people in the springtime sun. Our examining gaze passes over sunny grass, a brick sidewalk, a boot scraper, fluttering new leaves, bodies, and faces. They are configurations of black and grays on white, but our minds almost make the images breathe. We wonder what they are thinking. All we know about them is what we bring to them. And yet they touch us from somewhere beyond the mirror.

It must be early spring. The trees and shrubs show blossoms; the vines along the pillars begin to bloom. Leaves are not yet full. A small wind rustles the branches in the upper foreground. Maybe the man on the steps will go to war. He stands in the sunlight, his hair and beard golden for a moment. When he returns, *if* he returns, he will be iron. Who will he be then, where the others do not see? What is the cost of war to those who survive? Now he is a husband and father; then he will have killed his own kind.

See the little boy on the sidewalk. What will he pay, and who will he be that he is not? He is our grandfather or great-grandfather. What do we pay, and what might we have been, had not his father gone to war? Who are those people; what are we? See them looking at us from the mirror of time. "Who are you?" they ask. "What have we become in you?"

The Northerners had a difficult task in that war. They had to win it and virtually refuse to win it. They needed the South's cooperation, as Lincoln perceived, because the essence of the war was in people's hearts and minds. That is where the war began, and it would not be won only by physically defeating the South's armies. The war was about one section's unwillingness to remain part of the United States and participate in its institutions if the section's interests were jeopardized; it was about Americans participating in republican government. The essence of the revolt was in people's wills, just as the essence of republicanism is in voluntary agreement. The physical rebellion had to be put down, but the losers had to want to be United States citizens. Therefore the North had to act magnanimously, had to refuse to rub Southerners' noses in their defeat and disgrace, could not lecture them or abuse them, had to acknowledge Southern courage and brilliance, had to be careful about the underlying moral issue. Northerners could do this in a haphazard fashion eventually, though not at first, because they had never truly hated Southerners.

But Southerners had to respond to Northern good sportsmanship. Now, Southerners have never done well at playing games they don't like, so in secessionist fashion they proposed a different game. This one was successful. They declined to lose the war, while the North had to decline to win it.

At Appomattox, the ideal symbol of the way things should have worked was initiated by Joshua Chamberlain, the Union officer assigned to receive the surrender, and John B. Gordon, the Southern officer detailed to convey it. As Gordon dejectedly rode at the head of his exhausted column toward the lines of Union troops ready to receive their weapons, he heard the crisp Maine accents of Chamberlain's voice ordering his men to shoulder arms in a salute to their defeated former enemies. Looking up in momentary astonishment, Gordon quickly reacted in a way that epitomized what was best in the Old South. He reared his horse, and, drawing his sword in a high arc, touched its point to his boot tip in answering salutation. Salute answering salute, honor answering honor; it was one of the finest moments in American history.

But Northerners and Southerners were not up to it. The North, without the wisdom, practicality, and great-heartedness of Lincoln, proceeded to exercise their grief and rage on the prostrate South. Reconstruction took the course it did because many hearts had been broken. The South had made the war, and Northern families lived with vacant chairs in hundreds of thousands of their parlors as a result of it, along with hundreds of thousands of disabled and disfigured sons, fathers, and husbands. Congress waved the bloody shirt and passed punitive, vindictive laws. And profiteers knew how to make use of human feelings. Northern predators moved south.

So Southerners were confirmed, not contradicted, in their long-standing hatred of Northerners. This chronic antipathy was exacerbated by Carpetbaggers setting up what many Southerners perceived as uneducated, swaggering ex-slaves over them as representatives and local officials — with Yankee profiteers standing right behind them, of course, fat cigars clamped in their leering mouths as diamond-ringed fingers toyed with rolls of greenbacks. Such was the stereotyped image. Southern honor and Southern racial sensitivities smoldered. They had always detested Yankees, in part because Northerners self-righteously — hypocritically, Southerners added — reminded the South of their moral depravity in holding human beings as slaves. Southerners hated abolitionists the way you hate anyone who points out that something you are intimately attached to is wrong; but in this case it was more intolerable than that. Fear of slave rebellion raised the temperature, as it would not have had Southerners failed to understand that their property had every reason to feel rage. Furthermore, Southerners were moved by honor, and behind the abolitionist critique was the unavoidable implication that Southerners either were only nominal Christians, really greedy hypocrites, or they lacked the moral courage to free their three million slaves. The North was supposed to have a monopoly on greed — a fantastic but natural diversionary accusation deployed against factory owners and bankers by a group of people whose society and economy rested on human slavery. The North was also supposed to be the impious section, with its Unitarians and freethinkers and who knows what else that got off the boats from the slums and gutters of Europe. And Southerners did not permit their honor to be questioned.

In this we have the makings of a war, not the makings of peace. So those freed Negroes must be brought under control, and the South must not be seen to have lost the war fairly. For good measure, the moral upper hand must be claimed by reference to the dignity and spiritual grandeur of Southern leaders. All this happened, because the North never really hated the South and, like modern-day Americans who were victorious over Germany and Japan, they forgave their former enemies once the veterans got to reminiscing age. So the North acquiesced in the great mechanism that stated the conditions under which the Rebels would agree to become United States citizens. This mechanism is the Myth of the Lost Cause.

It is an attractive myth: it had to appeal to both sides in order to work. It is a retelling of the war by a people good at storytelling. It is a narrative which pictures the South as being not vanquished but overwhelmed — and not by human equals but by "numbers and resources." According to the myth, Southern troops always outfought their Northern opponents, always inflicted higher losses on the Yankees. Southerners had not started the war over the discredited institution of slavery, but over tariffs and irreconcilable cultural differences and the principle of states' rights. Finally, the Southern leaders and soldiers were cast as icons and placed in the pantheon of a popular religion.

The Northern people acquiesced because they felt less rancor than Southerners, because they had won, and because they moved on to the Gilded Age and then into the mad atmosphere of the twentieth century (someplace the South did not particularly want to go, often with good reason). Finally, the Myth of the Lost Cause — containing as one of its elements a romanticized picture of the Old South, the Antebellum South — was highly attractive to the white population. It was attractive as an escape from this mad century because it imagines a simpler time, because it is a wonderfully entertaining story of adventure and tragedy and romance and of a noble place and time now gone with the wind, because it shows Americans to be likable people and not too earnest or too inhumane, and because it camouflages the racism which persists in all sections of the country.

These are sizable benefits for great portions of the American population, but the benefits are only apparent. In reality, they are long-term liabilities and dangers, just as they were a century and a half ago. The first indication that this might be true is that the Lost Cause Myth is an insult thrown in the faces of most of those families who stare out at us from photographs of the Civil War era. It denies what they sent their sons and husbands to fight for and what their men died for. It denies those people their own principles, for which they gave the last full measure of devotion. It is as if we were to walk up the brick sidewalk to such a family as the one in the photograph — perhaps waiting on their porch for a soldier boy who will never return, and say to them that their boy went away and had a good fight and is now stone dead for no particular reason which would differentiate him from any other volunteer who ever went to war for what he believed.

Today, many Civil War buffs avoid the issues of the war by desiring to honor Southern soldiers in a vague and generic way for "fighting for their beliefs."[4] But Southern soldiers above all people would have hated being patronized. North and South, the men who fought the war would have wanted most for us to talk about whether their ideas were right or wrong. For them, those ideas justified their killing and dying. If neither side was wrong, could either side have been right? "If I was right," one of them might say, "do me the honor of commending me for it. If I was wrong, do me the justice of showing me, so I can own up and change." Until such a thing is done, the war remains unresolved. There will be no winners, not even ourselves — for whom many of them fought. I think you can love those guys without having to agree with all their ideas.

Facts have a function here in countering pernicious myths, but they once again operate as the bayonets of purpose. People use facts, and if they are to be used effectively, they must be marshaled within a more powerful myth than the one they attack. The question of myth is a question of people, and myth is closer than fact to why people start wars, why they fight wars, and what a war means when it is over.

Which myth expresses better the American identity — the Myth of the Lost Cause, or the Myth of National Redemption? Where did we come from, and where do we want to go? Who were those people back then? Which ones shall we choose to be our fathers and mothers? Who do we want to be?

All this is useful, even necessary, but it falls short of bringing us to a higher knowledge of the people we cannot seem to get along without. We choose our facts as we choose our myths, and determine what we want to be, using what we have made up about those people. But now we want to move on to a higher knowledge than knowledge of ourselves. Somehow we are drawn to those people. There is a kind of bond between us — not a mystic bond, but an everyday, simply human bond. In our own way and more than we know, we love those people. Why or how, we cannot say; but it is clear that we are incomplete without them. It is as if we were somewhere in that photograph with them. They have passed away and we are left with only the photograph. Funny, it is we who are missing.

Most people who are fascinated by the Civil War cannot explain their fascination. Having Civil War ancestors or living in Tennessee does not distinguish buffs from the uninterested. Nor does any amount of battlefield touring, artifact collecting, reenacting, or reading fully satisfy the longing that is the origin of one's interest. Such desire can be satisfied only by something as profound and personal as the longing itself. That is why partial knowledge based only on a selection and arrangement of facts can never be enough, nor will any myth fill the place of what is real. Both give us back only the image of our own minds. We study the generals, the battles, the armaments, and the economics of the Civil War only because such work lies within our poor power to maintain a tenuous connection with those people of the 1860s. We miss them in an uncanny and sentimental way, and we cannot get over it. The reality we crave is deeper and fuller than fact or fiction. To know it requires more than intellect or imagination; it requires our deepest capacity and calls forth the essence of who and what we are.

History is a poor substitute for the heaven in which those people believed. But like its cousin, Memory, History maintains an imperfect connection with those we love, and is easier for us to credit. Everyone dead and alive helps make us who we are. We know this. But those we love help to make us what we wish to be, and there is something of a heaven in that.

This family, in the way of families and in-laws, probably loves the young man on the steps. Perhaps he has volunteered for the army. And the young girl in the shawl might be gone from them before Christmas. Those who are left might gather sadly at the piano now and then in the evenings as people did in those days, and sing the old songs all of them once sang when they were together. One of them might be "Lorena":

> It matters little now, Lorena; the past is in th' eternal past.
> Our heads will soon lie low, Lorena; life's tide is ebbing out so fast.
> There is a future, O thank God! Of life, this is so small a part.
> 'Tis dust to dust beneath the sod, but there, up there, 'tis heart to heart.[5]

"Oh, what we might have been, Lorena!" It is the proverbial human cry of longing for the completeness and perfection this world and our natures do not permit. If we are to see our loved ones again, it must be in a heaven "up there." It cannot be here. Perfection does not exist here.

Here the conditions of life and our natures ensure that everything is sin. Though slavery is an abomination and the cause of secession was therefore "one of the worst for which people ever fought," Northerners were sinners, too, as Lincoln pointed out; and in any case, going out to kill another person, even to free the oppressed and safeguard liberty, is no innocent activity. So who is suitable for such a heaven "up there"?

Ethical dilemmas arise where perfection and imperfection meet, where this world stands before a pure world. The world of time strains toward a world to come. One kind of knowledge falters in the face of another; longing is an intimation of immortality. People in the trouble of war show us that love is the most exquisite pain and the highest form of knowledge. We can hope that it also makes imperfection pass away. We can hope that Dante was right: love not only moves the sun and the stars, it remakes us.

Reading this photograph is not easy. Perhaps the seated man is dark around his eyes, too. Is he the reason for the photograph's preservation? Did some collector mistake him for Abraham Lincoln, and thus the photograph bumbled its way into the archive?

Suppose we knew the facts. Suppose we knew each of these people's names. Suppose we knew everything: their birth dates; the location of the house; the day, month, and year. Suppose we knew the hour and minute the plate was exposed, and by whom. Suppose we knew whether the younger girl was seriously ill, and what her ailment was. We know what colors their dresses are, and of what materials they were made. We know when the house was built and how much it cost, where the older man worked and how much he earned, and the same for the younger man. We know their heights, the color of their eyes, and their weights, shoe sizes, hat sizes, and dress sizes. How many facts will do? If such facts are everything, then everything is nothing.

What difference does it make what their names are? What their ages are? The place, the time of day, what street they live on and in what state? We have lost them already. The remains of the bodies that made the photographic impressions lie in old graves now. We live in the tough and factual modern world. We cannot meet those people of the 1860s in our world. Nor do we seem able to meet them in theirs — that world where *there is a future, O thank God!* "O Heaven, whither?" writes Thomas Carlyle at the conclusion of *Sartor Resartus*. "Sense knows not; Faith knows not; only it is through Mystery to Mystery, from God and to God." If we ever see them face-to-face, it will be where time and times are done. They will call us by our true names, and we will know theirs. Their faces will no longer be reflections of our own minds. *Then I shall know, even as I am known.*

Witnesses

"I have never cried at Gettysburg, but I cried here this morning," a man told me the other day as we walked the Antietam battlefield. The sun was high and hot: summer baked the Sunken Road; the bronze and iron of plaques and monuments seemed to shimmer on fire. There was no shade. To witness an actual battle is the unconsidered wish of a Civil War student. But if it happened, if we finally saw what took place, it might be unbearable. Sometimes it does become almost real; sometimes you nearly understand what happened at some place on a battlefield, exactly where you are standing. You become a witness.

We saw no ghosts in that road, but knowledge became personal. An awful stillness filled the place. One does not speak in the presence of those dead — who seemed dead and alive at the same time. For that short time it felt as though two realities were interchanging, as though a wisp or shimmer of September 1862 was interlacing with the present afternoon. It was not at all like seeing ghosts; it was if intervening time had become compressed or had nearly vanished. In a timeless present, one can almost grasp what happened *here*, where hundreds of Confederates stood, and where hundreds of them died. Reenactors talk about a "period rush," but this was no rush. It was as if the dead lay around us, as if one could look at their faces. A face from a remembered photograph — such as the young Confederate lying beside the Hagerstown Pike fence some few hundreds of yards away — can summon the dead men, make it almost possible to stare at their stilled eyes, to almost touch the homespun cloth on one man's cold form.

> Somebody's darling, somebody's pride —
> Who'll tell his mother where her boy died?

The time between us vanishes, and we meet in the unconditional glare of the present. I see his powder-stained face and his open eyes. And now his Confederate cause haunts me more than he ever could have had he been a ghost.

"Battlefield mysticism": one who confesses to it abjures scientific, objective History, at least for a while. But I doubt whether there is such a thing as objective History. We are all haunted in one way or another, whether or not we comprehend what haunts us. Certainly, anyone who is not sentimental has no chance of understanding that war. Furthermore, if understanding involves more than factual knowledge, it also involves more than sentiment. If I am a witness for some young Confederate, having virtually seen his suffering, having stood strange vigil over his timeless body, I am somehow responsible for his cause.

To be responsible for a cause is not simply to fight for it blindly, which could be irresponsible; it is to understand that cause. The brave and defiant Confederate cause might have been — in the words U. S. Grant used in his memoirs — one of the worst causes a people ever fought for. Some of the causes of that Cause were not only honor and romanticism, but hatred and racism, self-interest and greed. To confess this, however, is only to give that young man his due. It is what we would want done for ourselves. If we are wrong, give us the chance to know it and repent. Yet that is the easy part. What haunts me is that I have missed something about the Confederate soldier, not only this one, but all the rest of them. Something more was in him, something my friend and I saw on that hot battlefield.

To be a witness, one must understand that facts are important. A witness represents facts. He or she is a living embodiment of facts and inhales and exhales the persistence of facts. A witness contradicts not only lies but also ignorance. So what I have said before about the limitations of facts presupposed that we have acquired not only a basic level of reliable information, but a good deal of it. To talk about issues and meaning, one has to have many facts and few misconceptions. Today, as any reader of *Confederates in the Attic* knows, many of us argue the issues and decide about meanings without knowing much.[1] A survey of Southern young people — the age of that young Confederate —

showed that only half of those people from the ages of eighteen through twenty-four could name a single battle of the Civil War.[2] Classroom guesses as to when slavery ended would appall Civil War buffs and should strike all Americans as not only shamefully ignorant but dangerous: "the 1900s" and "1940" came up in a class Horwitz witnessed, with the other students looking blank.[3]

But a fact is nothing when it is merely sat on. We use facts to reach understanding. To have seen a dead young Confederate in the Sunken Road was a personal experience, and now I must try to understand how my information intersects with his experience.

We have seen the faces of many dead Confederates. Think of Civil War photographs and Confederate dead come to mind. The photographers were usually Northerners and they came to Northern battlefields where the Union army had won the battles, controlled the fields, and had buried their own dead already. The killed Rebels still lay out under the hot sun. Something about this necessary neglect seems appropriate, because the photographs show ragged and famished men, orphans of the American Dream.

The Rebels were not only orphans of the material aspect of the American Dream; they were outsiders to the more fundamental aspect of the Dream: justice and equality for all. But this lack, too, on their part, is what reaches us about the dead Rebels.

They lie like abandoned rag dolls, sometimes stiff and numerous as cordwood — always numerous, it seems, which is part of that peculiarly indefinable tragedy and pathos of them — that deep, dark privacy only Southerners can really share. They died in prodigal numbers, though the Cause could not afford it. One-fourth of the Confederate men of military age died — a much higher percentage than in the North. The idea that Lee's men died in far lower numbers than the Army of the Potomac's men is probably sheer untruth, meant to bolster the Lost Cause axiom that Southerners outfought Yankees, but robbing us of something essential about those Rebels' sacrifice. They died in excess. They outdied the Yankees. They must have been on fire. It feels like the same fire that profligately and violently burns the stars.

They died hungry and in rags, died for a cause; they filled the Sunken Road on the Antietam battlefield, dead on dead so that a person could have walked the lane for a hundred yards without stepping on the ground — and then went on to die elsewhere on that battlefield after they were driven from the road. They died by the tens and hundreds, by the gross, in a stupid battle that never should have been fought — a battle that their enemies did not even do them the dignity of winning from them. A foolish Yankee commander refused to make the slaughter a victory. But from a historical point of view, the tactical stalemate at Antietam was one of the decisive events of the war: it forestalled foreign intervention and became the occasion for the Preliminary Emancipation Proclamation. These vital results were won over their dead bodies. Those Confederates were the obstacles, but somehow they have not come down to us as villains. In the photographs, those young Rebels have a strange innocence — an incorruptible condition more radically innocent than the innocence of birth. Did the wrong of their cause escape them with their last breath? Does pathos cover over their mistaken motives?

They did cherish some mistaken motives. If we want to make those boys prophets of freedom, new Sons of Liberty who refused to live under a government that interfered with individual or states' or counties' rights, we wind up trying to deny that slavery was the *sine qua non* of the War, the one thing without which none of this would have happened. I say as a witness who you might say nearly touched the hand of that young Confederate, who in a way has marched with him into this sunken road, that our boyish, rebellious opinions were mistaken and disastrous. Those who would make rebels with wrong causes into icons of freedom would deprive us of the one chance we have to make things right — to have died for something, to have learned. It would be to deprive us of rights more fundamental than self-government. And, as a witness, I must repeat that this young Confederate's death was not sweet and seemly. Yet I see him as somehow innocent.

> Somebody's darling, so young and so brave,
> Wearing still on his sweet yet pale face,
> Soon to be hid in the dust of the grave,
> The lingering light of his boyhood's grace.

Though the Yankee is my hero, the Confederate is my brother. I could apologize for him. It might even be true that the young Rebel was innocent of slavery, the way we, maybe, are innocent of the pollution that is destroying our children's world, or of any moral failure and laziness that our culture makes it extremely difficult to discern. To the young Rebel, slavery was as much a normal condition of life and a given circumstance as it was for Julius Caesar or George Washington or Saint Paul, or as it is for us to drive a car. So the Confederate died for slavery, but he did not die for slavery.

We are like him, which is one reason he is our brother. We most likely will die not for a noble cause but for nothing. We might be more wrong than right about what we believe. We are in general poorly led, and our sacrifice is only a sacrifice to fate, or to futility, or to meaningless humdrum. But what we see in the dead Confederates, dead by the thousand, is the very fire that we in our millions lack. "The mass of men lead lives of quiet desperation." So we stand our vigil at the flame, and cast the incense of our wonder on the fire.

Is it the fire of hate? No. Hate is a fuel perhaps, but not the fire: those Confederates are too sad, too innocent, too mysterious. Is it the fire of opinion, then? Perhaps such an idea comes closer, and yet we would have to delete the content of their opinions to reach that inexhaustible flame. In "A Prayer for My Daughter," William Butler Yeats writes:

> An intellectual hatred is the worst,
> So let her think opinions are accursed.
> Something essential and profound is left, when the storm of opinion
>   has passed.
> . . . all hatred driven hence,
> The soul recovers radical innocence . . .[4]

Today the opposite seems to be true. Today,

> The best lack all conviction, while the worst
> Are full of passionate intensity.[5]

To make our own use of the Confederates is to be bad witnesses and to kill them a second time. If they are to rise again, it is not their opinions that will be resurrected, nor will they put on our pet opinions like garments or masks. They will regard us face-to-face, with the innocence of summer stars.

We reenact Civil War battles, marches, and encampments because we still wish to be witnesses to those people. We read the books and visit the memorials because we are witnesses. Today, with tens of thousands of reenactors, and angry men and women all over the country thinking they would be happier if only Confederate opinions had won, the Civil War seems to be a time whose idea has come. But that is not why we are witnesses, why we can hardly help but be witnesses.

> Tenderly bury the fair, unknown dead,
> Pausing to drop on his grave a tear.

Carve on the wooden slab over his head,
"Somebody's darling is slumbering here."

Most of us, even those who feel affection for the Confederates, affirm the Union cause when we consider the matter. Visiting the battlefields, we admire those Northern men who offered their lives to prevent this country from dividing, and we are thankful. Without them, would we and our children be enjoying this beautiful country? If this country had turned into two antagonistic nations, the twentieth century would not have been the American Century; it would have been Hitler's Century or the Soviet Century. If we cannot forget the Civil War, neither ought we to remember it the wrong way. Still, the War reflects to us our hopes and angers, our dreams and our pains. We invest it with the "what ifs" of our own lives.

The Civil War looks back at us like a mirror. The Union soldier shows us what we ought to be; the Confederate shows us what we are. The unfulfilled dream retains its painful place in us. The Confederate hunger is our hunger; their rage is our rage. Their flame still burns — their devotion to a cause no one can define, their gallant and calamitous waste, their fury to perpetuate what never was, their lives thrown down in useless defiance of the best conditions in this world, their ravenous devotion and their longing.

What you see in those dead Confederates is not only the spent fuel of a flame but the flame itself. If the South ever rises again it will not be the political or geographical South that immolated itself in a rash and destructive rebellion. What rises from the ashes could only be a new incarnation of the indomitable and tragic will to refute the limitations of human life. Such will be the epic of the Confederacy if it is ever written for all time.

On the Antietam battlefield, my friend asks me a question: "Which side would you fight for?" It is not a childish question, merely an impossible one. Everything would be different if it were 1862. The person I am now could not answer. A great chasm has been fixed between the people of the 1860s and us, and we could not recognize them with the eyes of 1862 even if one of them were to come back from the dead. Yet somehow, perhaps, a way exists to know them. Those who are unable to let those people go, unable to let them drop into the dark forgetfulness at the bottom of that abyss, have started to walk the ghost road with them.

If it were to happen again today and one had to choose the side to fight on, and if joining either army would not be an unacceptably evil thing, most patriotic modern Americans would choose the Army of the Republic. Yet as those ragged gray and butternut lines came on, those jaunty scarecrows dying under our muskets and artillery, would we have the heart to shoot? It would be like shooting roses, like shooting stars down from the sky. And still they would come on, fierce and hungry and yelling their high wail. Do they burn in heaven, as they did here? Will it all be made beautiful somehow?

But if you were a Yankee at the Hagerstown Pike, you would not have enjoyed the luxury of sentimentalizing the Rebel just now pointing his gun. Those Rebels over there are not stars or roses. They are enraged enemies who have made their decision. "For their beliefs" they intend to kill you and your friends. You fire.

There he lies. Between his stiffening fingers he holds a photograph. See his wife and child. A hundred fifty years from now, enthusiasts of this war will want to be in your place. Yes, this is the Rebel you killed the day before yesterday. He's black and swollen. This isn't a husband and father now; this is a foul-smelling rotten thing. And they will weep for this mother's darling who was running to drive his bayonet through your heart.

When the past becomes present, pictures in the imagination become reality and abstraction becomes horror. Political and philosophical errors become visible evil. They become men firing bullets and corpses lying in the road. When the wished-for reality of the Civil War appears to the historian or buff or battlefield visitor, however ephemerally, the nostalgic beauty of that old time is replaced by cruelty. Where monuments stood, ghastly figures scream at their own blood; national issues assume the terrible willfulness of the god of war; books and reasoning vanish as the struggle becomes personal. Finally one understands the essential thoughts of Civil War soldiers in general: This is simply awful; God help me. War is no longer a mere object of study but a brutal act done by one person against another. "The Bonnie Blue Flag" and "The Battle Cry of Freedom" are gone and we can think only of the soldiers' favorite, "Home, Sweet Home," because the Civil War was hell on earth. To that, the battlefield seer is a witness.

"... You Cannot Refine It."

The fields were turning ripe that sunny afternoon in Gettysburg. New, long grass flourished green, springing limber and strong in rows and acres and multitudes. A full summer's heat lay ahead, and the pale desiccation of late fall, but now the soft rains of spring had only just ceased, and the tender grass of the field raised its juicy blades to the sun.

A fitful west breeze carried the faint thrill of fife and drum. Tourists near the High-Water Mark began to hear it, and one by one, in groups and families, they migrated to the stone wall. Looking west across the fields in front, across the Emmitsburg Road toward the far edge of the wide fields where Generals Pickett and Pettigrew had formed their lines, you could see a tiny group gathering into formation. Its flags went up — the thrill of it passed through the crowd where we now stood, still and attentive. It must be a full company of reenactors, about to follow the path of Pickett's Charge. Distance gave the sight a strange and exciting authenticity. They would be coming toward us, all the way across those fields.

Yet now they enacted the realistically aggravating delay attendant upon military maneuvers. At our great distance, we could barely make out the forms of officers moving back and forth behind and before what was probably a double line of men. They were causing the lines to be dressed, aligning them, realigning them, ordering the proper intervals and spacing. You might barely make out the thin voices of shouting officers — but no, they were too far away. The fifes and drums had ceased.

Now they resumed. The lines began to move. On they came, distant and minute, but steady. Two flags waved in front at the center, though from this far they seemed only to rise to the height of the men. Officers marched at both sides, in front, and behind, swords probably unsheathed. Behind them, a smaller group barely visible, beating out the steady drum rattle and fifing a still-indistinguishable tune.

The line would not reach us for fifteen or twenty minutes, yet none of the crowd at the wall became restless or drifted away. More tourists came up, attracted by our numbers, then lifted their gaze across the fields and saw the narrow mass of approaching men, heard the nineteenth century martial music, a little more audible now but small on the uncertain breeze. All stood in quiet attentiveness.

Pride, an unusual sensation, swelled a little among us. You could feel it in that silent attention. A glimpse of honor, a palpable reminiscence of devotion, a clear evidence of discipline — and the flag, coming across the field. It was the United States flag; the men were uniformed in dark blue. One's heart swelled a little. One remained, waited, to honor what the banner stood for, to pay devotion to devotion, as a faithful gesture of respect offered to the memory of those steadfast men of 1863. For these moments, their discipline will be our discipline. For a time, we will lay aside our wishes, our schedules, our desires — as they did. It is the very least we can do. And it makes us proud, if only a little, to do it. For a while, each of us is one of them.

And to augment the honor, these men in blue were following the footsteps of the men in gray. Somehow it did not matter, here at the wall, what state any of us was from, or which army our interests and affections sided with. Here the men in blue under Old Glory retracing the Confederate advance had become all armies, all soldiers everywhere — marching under the clear, bright sky, through the bowing grain.

Several of the older men at the wall removed their baseball caps. A child in a carrier strapped in front tugged her mother's collar and pointed — she could see them now. Her curls reminded me of the Civil War song:

> One little curl from its golden mates take,
> Somebody's pride it was once you know . . .

But looking at those men marching toward us with determination and strength caused me to wonder whether the innocence of Civil War soldiers was not exaggerated, a result of 1860s sentimentality and our own. Perhaps the Somebody's Darling of the song, whose golden curls were once a mother's pride, was the Rebel who pointed his gun at a blue soldier boy trying to comfort his mortally wounded officer at Gettysburg and growled, "Get to the rear, you damn Yankee son of a bitch!" or perhaps he was the Union boy who shot the Southern good Samaritan in front of the wall at Marye's Heights as he went from wounded man to wounded man with his canteen. If it is true that America before the Civil War was an innocent country, then a worse tragedy than the deaths of "sweet, pale" boys was the mad extinguishing of the "lingering light of boyhood's grace." Yet a terrible beauty was born, the turning of boys into men of iron determination, the genesis of valor and steadfastness that can make or preserve a nation.

The steady line had about reached the fences along the Emmitsburg Road. In firm unison they halted. We could hear harsh shouts from the officers. The two lines evolved into a double column. They were not going to scramble over the fence as Pickett's men had; they were forming up and marching for an open place in the fence line. Cars on the Emmitsburg Road stopped as the blue column came through. The flags led, crossing the road and aiming for the open section on this side of the road. Behind them, the fifes and drums, silent. We could see the musicians distinctly enough now to count them: three drummers, three pipers.

Now their column had entered the field in front of us, and, under the harsh commands of their officers, the men filed off by the left, evolving again into the double line of battle. The flags stopped in the center. Once again, like Pickett's men, the company dressed its lines and evened its spacing under the cold eyes of its officers. Now again the drums in the clear air, the fifes playing; and the lines move forward up the field. Again a thrill fills our hearts at the wall.

We are now gathered two or three deep. More people hurry toward us. Young couples watch fixedly; several families, children gathered in front, stare in admiration; a group of Cub Scouts assembles in awe. The discipline of the company in blue is flawless and impressive. They do not hurry, do not cheer or shout or talk; they do not rush. Steady at a walk, they march right up toward our guns, stopping once again not thirty yards away to dress their lines perfectly, the officers demanding a halt. Waving and pointing their swords, the officers call out their stern orders. "Close up, there!" "Fill that gap!" I notice now that the officers are all taller than the enlisted men . . . and now for the first time I perceive that *the soldiers are all children*. Around them, men in their fifties strut and bark — the boys and girls obeying their orders frightened but proud, their faces stiff. The fifty-year-olds dressed up like officers stalk along the lines, proud and imperious and exacting. Children! Not men, not reenactors, but children. Here at last is the image I wanted — the clear, perfect image of war.

I feel virtually sick. I wanted to see war and here it is. I walk away from the stone wall. I avoid the eyes of tourists hurrying the other way. Behind me, the fifes and drums sound. I do not look. The lines are moving again, orderly and proud, right up to the stone wall; the crash is coming; the old men lift their chins and point their swords; the flags rush forward. I know it now. *War is cruelty . . .*

The Road to Gettysburg

I.
Soldiers passed along this road, where snow
of apple blossoms blows. But in their time
it was high summer, and the careless rhyme
of their confederacy was half told.
Sweet white petals cover their intentions
and their dust. On other roads their enemies
approached, and all the epic conventions
old Homer handed down demanded battle.
Men must bleed. Soon musketry's hot rattle
put lead to kill two armies into Gettysburg's trees.

Who knows now if the angry vanished sang
the marching harmonies of their beliefs,
or lavished the last leisure of their griefs
on sweet songs full of lavender and pangs?
The muse exhales across her tender lips
in singing. All's metered, and no verse is free
if free means measureless, for we
are mortal, marking time foot by short foot.
The bugler spends his breath with reveille
and closes all the lonely notes of taps.

Both armies sought the felon dignity
of triumph as they passed along their ways,
for killers masquerade in history
as saints, and poets lie because a lie
is prettier than death. How much bad faith
lies buried in the songs is anybody's guess —
the marching songs that give a lilt to wrath
and organize the awful, meaty mess
of war, and sentimentalize the smell
of what is left after we descend to hell.

The Rebels brought their shadows up this road,
murmuring by thousands to be free:
the weary men who bore the weary load
of war. Such is the price of poetry.
"Swing low, sweet chariot" scarce dared the air
to carry it among so many guns,
but its rhythms measured all the soldiers there.
For is he slave or free, that summer sun,
who sheds his flame like bleeding men shed prayers,
with nothing to do but roam around heaven all day?

Gettysburg is now a place for pilgrims.
In summer all the roads are swelled again.
The long ago is lyricized; the dim
Republic trembled in the breath of men.
Only the damned can make a paradise
of hell. The soldiers' ode to Gettysburg
was never sung, and yet we listen for the words.
We are more imaginative than wise.
The wrath was too much for our touchy eyes:
we concentrate on landscape, trees, and birds.

But soldiers weathering that sacred storm
amid red questions only God can ask
and get an answer, handled their unfinished task
as if it wouldn't do us any harm.
The years have told. What they have made
seems better than anything they did. Strange
and beautiful are some things forced of flesh
and blood. It seems that only God refreshes

the dead, or makes a paradise of hell,
or loads a lyric in an iron shell.

II.
This year it is the driest spring recorded;
the orchards thirst, and all the fields need rain.
Nature's ways can hardly be afforded,
but lilacs bloom in dooryards yet again.
A bluebird sings. A redwing blackbird scolds
and launches out upon a dodging sparrow,
shoots up and down around a little circle
in the warming air. A sweet fragrance drifts
from clover in the fields, white and purple;
an angry cloud of gnats descends and lifts.

A songbird lifts its little cape of black
and white, declining from a fencepost down
into the grass, uniting with its shadow.
Up rush a couple of butterflies, white
and yellow, and they flutter so alarmed
and close, it seems they clash. If this is harm,
let life be for such harm, for now they rise —
the lyric of their rising carries them so high —
revolving and ascending — lost to sight —
that everything resolves into that flight.

The armies' roads led straight to Abraham
Brian's house on Cemetery Ridge. Black
and free, the family was gone when Lee,
for the lost cause of rights and liberty,
decided that small home was the place to attack.
They weren't much better served by Uncle Sam,
who gave the Brians fifteen on the thousand
for damages. Two small rooms, nothing more —
four chairs, two beds, a table, stove, washstand:
the less you have the more you give to war,

until the only thing you have is life,
and war wants that. The black and white of it
on Cemetery Ridge — the children, wives,
and parents struck — is one sad balance sheet.

One looks into the Brians' windows now
and wonders what such lives are for: so poor
they lived but to survive — one wonders how —
and could not lock, nor needed lock, their door.
What's kept from moth and rust will go to theft.
They had each other. Nothing else is left.

III.
And so the soldiers molding in their graves.
The soiling stories of the dead and bold
are bravery's immortality — if told.
The cause has had its day. Nothing is saved.
The words they sang when marching on this road
have gone to different songs. The farmer's plow
will ride the roofs of cities. Nothing's old.
The marble monument, the sweetest ode,
shall crumble in the bosom of the Lord.
There is a different drummer now.

Then what is life, and what are battles for?
What lasts, or why should lasting matter?
The buttons on the shirt you're buried in
will outlast brain and heart and hands and skin.
What matters what the goal or which the road?
Why should the poet care who reads his ode
or when? The soldiers who have gone above,
to hell, to worms — the fools, the dutiful —
have left something that almost feels like love,
a battlefield that now is almost beautiful.

A mother lifts her tiny toddler's fists
a-walking in the Soldier's Cemetery.
"Show me thy paths, Lord," sang the wandering psalmist.
So all soldiers learn to walk. "Show me thy way."
No headstones tell the saviors from the saved:
"The paths of glory lead but to the grave."
Here at last are sown the soldier's bones
found late alone. "Civil War Remains"
reads the still-pristine stone. The poet Gray
would muse upon the name: simply "Unknown."

On a Minnesota grave there rests a rose
today, upon a stone that reads "Unknown" —
a lyric note whose tone nobody knows,
left for the unknown by the unknown.
The tired and angry come to Gettysburg
to lay their questions at the fading feet
of those who struggled here before. A word
of recognition sounds as sweet
as ever. The troubled pass their prayers away,
and walk through paradise their solitary ways.

A boney old man scavenging cans alone
leans tired on an iron canister
and rests. This may be paradise for some.
Just beyond that hill the field is summer;
Longstreet's regiments, now ready, call
down the folly and the horror of the hour.
Tense Philadelphia men wait at the wall.
The blowing roses kindle into flower.
So all is wasted, all is spent; and all
the wrath of war is buried where it falls.

IV.
Out of the mash and hell of that bloodbath —
up from the waste that always rewards wrath —
a union bloomed more perfect than before.
The strangely faithful veterans returned,
their graying heads still full of youth and war,
to see again those others who had burned
with that necessity, had sung the songs,
had executed orders all too well,
had wrought the same ungodly wrongs —
and left here something very unlike hell.

The road to Gettysburg is violet
this evening as the tired, rose-red sun sets.
"The Battle Cry of Freedom" stirs their hearts
and "Home, Sweet Home" may sweeten their regrets.
In thirty years, survivors in their fifties
will hear sons harmonize "Daisy, Daisy"
and "Sweet Adeline," differently crazy,

---

and watch their children going off to war,
happy not to ask what this one's for —
but oh, the thought of brothers gone before.

We're all here now, the living and the slain:
the fallen couples stroll their wandering ways
through Eden. If the past were rhymed and sung
instead of suffered, and if the right
were always sweeter than the wrong,
what gentle music and what sacred light
would soothe and radiate our dreams.
The battlefield would be a place to walk at night,
and all would be as harmless as it seems:
all lyrical, no musketry, no screams.

Leaves here are not quite vegetable gold,
no perfect pair is here to cultivate;
the tree of knowledge has been marked and cut,
and its fruits continue to be sold.
Still, in the cool of evening someone walks
like some good shepherd among still flocks.
Deep music from a vastness beyond words
is seldom understood but often heard.
One could remain, remain and roam these bright fields always;
one could ignore that terrible swift sword.
But sweet and seemly as it feels to stay,
the God of Battle marches us away.

Epilogue

Les Terribles

He came when they called him. That is the kind of man he was. He would always help out not because he did not have anything else to do, but because you needed something done. If you had measured wrong trying to hang a door, it was no use trying to apologize to him when he showed up. "Aw hell," he'd grunt. "What was I doing so damn important I couldn't leave it for an hour?" He could do, and had done, quite a few things, like many men and women who grew up on farms during the Great Depression. After leaving the farm he had driven a truck, done carpentry, and tended bar. As a bartender he was a natural. You could talk to him about anything for hours on end and get good common sense and plenty of stories in return. Some of them were farm stories, but most of them were war stories.

There was the time he was carrying in a case of bandoliers, for instance, and forgot the password. The Japanese were only a quarter of a mile away and the men on guard duty were in no mood to make exceptions. The officer in charge had him led over, ordered him to sit down, and asked him to name all the teams in the Big Ten while looking into the barrel of a loaded revolver. "That damn Purdue. That was the one I couldn't think of," he said. His questioners had little patience for hesitation on this point. All the men of the Red Arrow Division were from Wisconsin or Michigan, Big Ten states, and if you couldn't name the football teams in that conference, you were a Japanese infiltrator no matter what you looked like. Dick tried to think of that tenth team and the officer said, "Anybody here vouch for this guy? You got ten seconds." Somebody stepped into the little group and said, "That's Benson. I know him." The officer lowered his revolver and said, "Soldier, you don't know how lucky you are." Dick rose to his feet and said, "The hell I don't."

My thesis is that it is actually *we* who are the lucky ones, but meanwhile Dick went back to the war and helped win it. The 32d "Red Arrow" Division saw more combat than any other American division in the Pacific — 654 days of actual fighting — and its men received 11,500 Purple Hearts. That was about the original number enrolled. Dick had been saved from summary execution because a lot of those fighting men knew him. Knew him and liked him.

You could not help liking Dick. He was the epitome of the World War II American soldier: solid, enduring as an army mule but always full of fun, and, above all, decent. I realize that decency is a comparative term. You don't always do decent things in 654 days of combat. Still, while the overrun peoples of World War II dreaded and feared the Germans, the Russians, the Japanese, and even the French, they were usually happy to see Americans coming. The GIs would give them food, candy, and cigarettes, not rape their women, and not shoot their old men. Decent. They were decent in a very indecent world. They were also the kind of guys who, if they came into a village and found a live phone line, would try to get through to Emperor Hirohito himself and tell the son-of-a-bitch to expect them in about a week. That is something Dick and his buddies would have done. (It actually *was* done by a GI in Europe, who, although unable to reach Hitler, did manage to talk to someone in the German high command.)

What was unique about Dick was the rakish gleam in his eye, the raffish grin that accompanied it. And he was a handsome devil, young Benson. But, you see, it was that rakish gleam coupled with a solid, fundamental decency that everybody understood, which made him stand out. You would trust your life to him. He did not have a dishonest bone in his body. He would not take advantage of you if you were the dumbest Swede in Christendom. He would turn all the young women's heads — he looked like Douglas Fairbanks Jr. with his slick black hair and thin moustache. But he took no liberties and he stayed on the straight and narrow, just as boys were brought up to do in western Wisconsin. And when they called him up, he went with the obligatory complaint but never even considered staying behind — even though he had a pretty young wife at home.

Just like when we called him that Sunday morning — or, strictly speaking, when my mother or dad called him, for the young fellow he was helping out was me, by agreeing to be my godfather. I was eight years old, an odd age to be baptized, but if the idea was to do it so that I would remember, it worked. The planned godfather had been suddenly called in to work, so Dick showed up in his place. It was like having the Rock of Gibraltar behind you. I was a little afraid of him then, although our family and his had been friends since long, long before I came along. Just about six feet tall, still wearing the thin moustache, a no-nonsense look on his face: he stands over me next to the baptismal font in a black-and-white photograph. I still tend to see him in black and white. He was a giant to me then, and he is a giant to me now.

As I have implied, Dick had not been lounging around with noth-ing to do that Sunday. He was working two jobs at the time. Weekdays, he was a guard at the Stillwater State Penitentiary, across the river. Among the many tough jobs Dick was ideal for, prison guarding must have stood out. Dick was one tough man and nobody dared give him any nonsense. At the same time, he treated everyone like a human being, prisoner and officer alike — a quality that earned him not the mere imitation respect accorded to strong men, but genuine admiration and trust. Evenings and weekends, Dick and his wife Mary ran a grocery store. It was small, in a bad location, and they did not have enough cash to invest in much to stock the spacious shelves. Before long, the store winked out. They looked for another place to live, again (the store had been their home); Mary found part-time work copyediting the local newspaper, and Dick worked odd jobs to pay for the house. Still, from that year onward, they always sent me a birthday card with two dollars in it, the equivalent of twenty today or perhaps a hundred, from people who worked hard and long hours to pay their obligations. With unfail-ing regularity, Mary and Dick showed they had not forgotten the special obligation that had been imposed by chance, fate, or God, through the call of duty.

I came of age during a war when the call of duty was not clear. Was it our duty to go over to Vietnam and fight, or was it our duty to stop a war that many said was indecent and foolish? Dick never spoke about this war to me, but concerning the men fighting it, he had his opinions. When he learned that American soldiers had shot civilians or burned villages, he would not even accord that behavior the time wasted on an expression of contempt. True, the world had changed and right and wrong were not the same as they had been in the 1940s, perhaps, but don't bother trying to tell him that. Killing civilians violated the sense of decency that was as much a part of him as an indelible metallic aroma is a part of steel. Never mind that Americans had bombed civilians during the war Dick had fought in himself.

The decency of the men of his generation offers an insight into one of the greatest mysteries of the Civil War. I should mention here that the 32d Red Arrow Division was the direct descendant of the Civil War's Iron Brigade. In 1917, the 2d Wisconsin, an organization dating back to the first battle of Bull Run, was stationed on the Mexican border with some other Wisconsin and Michigan units. America's entry into the European war in 1917 caused these troops and others to be formed into the 32d Division, which soon embarked for France. Those men, descendants of the Iron Brigade geographically, organizationally, biologically, and otherwise, were in turn the military fathers of Dick's 32d Red Arrow Division of the Second World War, a division that lived up to its lineage.

The originals, the Iron Brigade, suffered more casualties than any other Union formation of its size in the Civil War, at a time when high casualties resulted not from ineptitude but from standing and fighting. That unit also *inflicted* more casualties than any other Union brigade — considerably more casualties than it received. If the Iron Brigade was not the best brigade in the Civil War, it is unclear which one was. And its soldiers would have been satisfied with their figurative grandson, Dick Benson, and his friends in the 32d Division.

Likewise, Dick's character and that of his messmates provides an answer to one of the most important questions of the Civil War. I have claimed that the American GI was a decent young man. Historians aplenty could rush forward to point out exceptions. Likewise, Civil War soldiers deserted now and then, resorted to prostitutes here and there, stole and lied on occasion. The generalization, "American soldiers were decent," is a generalization, meaning there were exceptions, and meaning that the claim is applied comparatively. A generalization is no more than that — but it is also no less.

Sherman's march through Georgia is good evidence in favor of this generalization. The march was an outrage, and still is, when considered from the Southern viewpoint — but only because the rules of warfare were comparatively decent at the time. You did not threaten civilians or destroy their livelihoods. War was to be waged by soldiers against soldiers only. So the background of Sherman's march was, militarily speaking, decent. Even if you consider the violators themselves, Sherman's boys, you come out with a picture of comparative decency. No murders were committed, virtually no rapes, and if there were exceptions, they were just that — exceptions. In others words, Sherman's boys were a lot more decent than you and I might be under similar circumstances.

But the point is that Sherman's march was *indecent* by Civil War standards. They had high standards. And here is a solution to the great mystery: Why did Union soldiers fight? The question of why Southern soldiers fought is a comparatively easy riddle. Some question how people could have fought hard and long for a cause contaminated by slavery. However, slavery was not considered a contaminant but a way of life by the Confederacy's white population. You and I might fight for our way of life. Abraham Lincoln himself stated that had he been in the Southerners' position, he probably would have done exactly as they were doing. Most of all, Southerners fought because they valued their honor above all things and felt intolerably offended by Northerners, upon whom they wasted no affection and whom they considered to be inferior. Then, too, the South was being invaded. Most people will fight invaders, no matter what the cause on either side.

But the North was not being invaded. The Northern way of life would not have been destroyed by successful secession. Northerners did not detest Southerners. Why, then, did they wage a long offensive war, necessitating higher casualties than a defensive war; and how could they conquer an area larger than Napoleon had, without the three-to-one advantage experts say should have been required to assure victory? The answer is that the Union soldier was not only as brave as the doughboy and GI of the world wars; he was as decent, or more so. The Union soldier fought to save what he thought was the best government on earth because it was the only guarantor of liberty for posterity; and some, mostly New Englanders, also fought to free other men and women. In general, preserving the Union was a decent cause, as causes go. Do not tell me that Yankees fought merely to keep slaves from competing with free labor, any more than that GI's fought to keep their Fords and Chevrolets. When Southerners seceding from the Union fired upon the flag, and the president wanted troops to enforce the laws, enlisting was the decent thing to do for many Northern young men. The Union cause, and the expeditions to Europe and the Pacific in which Southerners and Northerners alike fought in the twentieth century, were crusades in whatever positive sense might be summoned for the word.

Decency is hard to define. Southerners thought Northerners to be an indecent lot, and abolitionists could not imagine decent people keeping slaves. The dictionary helps only a little: *decent* means "to be characterized by conformity to recognized standards of propriety and morality." Further, an individual decent to the core is usually seen as an exception among men and women, not a common type in any era. It is only by reference to a generally less decent era, like ours, that an earlier time appears to be decent. The Civil War had its Abraham Lincoln and, some would add, Robert E. Lee, who stood out from the rest of their contemporaries. But Billy Yank and GI Joe stand apart from us. I am not saying that we are lost; I am saying that we are lucky. These men were our fathers.

The Civil War's Iron Brigade was composed of three Wisconsin regiments and one from Indiana. After the Battle of Antietam, the 24th Michigan was added to the brigade, which in four closely spaced battles had lost three-quarters of its men. They had lost one-third at Brawner Farm, facing a reinforced Stonewall Division and inflicting twice their own losses on Jackson's men. The brigade formed the Union army's rear guard at Second Manassas, and earned the name "Iron Brigade" at South Mountain by attacking a securely placed enemy up a steep, wooded slope. Three days after losing one-fourth of their reduced number at South Mountain, the brigade's remaining eight hundred men were chosen to lead the Union attack on Lee's left flank across Antietam Creek. D. R. Miller's now-famous "Cornfield," through which the Iron Brigade attacked on the morning of September 17, 1862, became some of the most "bloody, dismal" acres in the history of modern warfare.

At dawn, the four regiments went forward to the Miller farm buildings, drove off the Confederate skirmishers positioned there, and advanced into a field of corn that towered over the men's heads. They could see nothing, but the mounted officers behind them could see sunlight glinting off dense rows of bayonets at the opposite end of the field. Two Confederate brigades were waiting. The killing began when a Confederate shell exploded in the ranks of the advancing 6th Wisconsin, cutting through eleven men.

As his four regiments went forward, Brig. Gen. John Gibbon, the brigade commander, saw that three more Confederate brigades were advancing out of a woods off to the right front. If they were not stopped, they would strike the brigade's right flank and overwhelm it. Now outnumbered three or four to one, Gibbon divided his brigade, sending two regiments across a road to engage the flanking Confederates, and two regiments plunging straight ahead into the tall corn. On the right, the 7th Wisconsin and 19th Indiana not only charged the Southerners but also succeeded in throwing them back, forcing them into the woods.

The conflict quickly became a "storm" of bullets, shells, and solid shot through which the Wisconsin men charged. Knapsacks, arms, rifles, and heads were tossed into the air, gruesomely wheeling and falling. Firing with "demoniacal" fury and speed, shouting and laughing in the hysteria of battle, the 2d and 6th Wisconsin struck the heavier Confederate line, which began streaming to the rear as a second line of Union troops caught up with the Iron Brigade. Seeing the retreating Confederates pour back past a small white church, the Wisconsin men, exhausted but wild with excitement, reordered themselves into line of battle and charged again.

However, as they moved toward the church, a new body of Rebels emerged from the woods behind it. This long line consisted of two brigades that blasted a sheet of fire at the surprised Wisconsinites, cutting them down "like a scythe," one of the 6th's officers reported. One Confederate brigade moved off toward the Iron Brigade's left flank, encountering other Union troops. John Bell Hood's Texans, overlapping the two Wisconsin regiments, pushed straight forward. The 2d and 6th retreated to the Cornfield and tried to maintain their line. They found that many of their rifles would no longer fire, having become hot and fouled during the terrible advance through the field. Now they walked back through the shattered rows of corn, firing if possible, men dropping with every yard, the disintegrating line uncovered.

Across the road, officers of the 7th Wisconsin and 19th Indiana saw what was happening to their sister regiments. These men had not pursued the Confederates they had defeated, so as the Texans advanced on the other side of the road and came abreast of them, the 7th and 19th wheeled at a right angle and charged. Though it was only two spent regiments against a full fresh brigade, the shock of an unexpected flank attack shattered the Texans' left and forced the entire brigade to fall back. Now the 6th and 2d halted their retrograde movement and, one more time, charged through the Cornfield.

The fighting was so violent and confused, so filled with crashes, screams, and smoke, that one survivor wrote that it seemed like a "tumbling together of all heaven and earth." Heavy slugs fired at such close range caused men not to fall but to be knocked off their feet when hit, an officer wrote. Confederate artillery, massed in front and on the right, got the Wisconsin and Indiana men in a crossfire. And then, as the battered Iron Brigade reached the south end of the Cornfield again, they saw more troops: a fresh brigade of the enemy along with reformed units of the previously encountered Confederate brigades. These joined Hood's men, and they and the Texans came on again.

Once more it was back through the Cornfield, which by then was a flat field trashed with fragmented cornstalks, all the equipment of men at war, and covered by fallen soldiers in blue and gray. After it was over, an officer said that the field looked as if the stalks had all been cut at the ground with a knife. Through this, the Wisconsin men retreated.

Only one battery of artillery was immediately available to support the Union troops in the Cornfield. General Gibbon, who had once been Battery B's commander, saw that many of its men and horses were down. Leaping from his saddle, he aimed one of its guns, double-shotted with canister, at Confederates who had advanced to within a few yards. The general depressed the tube as far down as it would go. Ricocheting up off the ground right in front of the piece, the iron canister balls sprayed through the Texans, and a whole rank of men went down. The Cornfield was not only a shambles, it was stained and almost running with blood.

By midmorning, both sides had been fought out and the Cornfield was a no-man's-land, as the blasted space between trenches would be called forty-five years later in the World War. The Iron Brigade had lost 42 percent of its men. The Confederates had been made to suffer substantially worse. One Rebel brigade lost 48 percent, including five of six regimental commanders; another lost 60 percent, with all its colonels down; another lost 30 percent, including three of its four regimental commanders. These Southern brigades had fought in the Cornfield. Across the road, three more Confederate brigades had lost heavily. In front of Battery B, served by many infantrymen of the Iron Brigade, lay a "mass of dead Confederates." With good reason, Bruce Catton and Alan Nolan called the Iron Brigade "the shock troops of the Army of the Potomac." Had a group of World War I French officers been present to watch, surely they would have called these Iron Brigade men *"Les Terribles."*[1]

[]

Fifty-two years after the Civil War, the 2d and 6th Wisconsin were once again on active duty. Together with four other Wisconsin regiments, they formed half of one of the new "Pershing divisions" being trained for France. The other half of the division consisted of Michigan troops. As the brigade had been the basic combat unit of the Civil War, so the division became the basic unit of the American Expeditionary Force (AEF), under the command of Gen. John J. Pershing. After three years of horrific stalemate on the western front, which stretched in an unbroken line of trenches from the North Sea to the Swiss border, the Allies were counting on the eventual arrival of millions of American troops to turn the war against Germany. Pershing organized big divisions: each AEF division was twice the size of a European division. But could Americans fight? Yanks began arriving in the spring of 1917, but it was anticipated that the American army would take nearly two years to reach full strength. The Allies hoped that with 3 million Americans in Europe to act as replacements in veteran French and British units, they could win sometime in 1920.

In February 1918, the Wisconsin and Michigan troops of the 32d Division arrived in France, the sixth of what was planned to be an AEF force of well over a hundred divisions. The German high command was not interested in waiting for American numbers to weigh in against them, however, and in March they began a huge, powerful offensive against the French and British line. In May, part of the 32d Division was sent to a French corps that had been decimated by German assaults.

The Midwestern boys were now introduced to the unprecedented horror of World War I trench warfare. A British officer compactly described the kind of experience the Europeans had perpetrated and endured for the past three years:

> the leprous earth, scattered with the swollen and blackened corpses of hundreds of young men. The appalling stench of rotten carrion. . . . Mud like porridge, trenches like shallow and sloping cracks in the porridge — porridge that stinks in the sun. Swarms of flies and bluebottles clustering on pits of offal. Wounded men lying in the shell holes among the decaying corpses: helpless under the scorching sun and bitter nights, under repeated shelling. Men with bowels dropping out, lungs shot away, with blinded, smashed faces, or limbs blown into space. Men screaming and gibbering. Wounded men hanging in agony on the barbed wire, until a friendly spout of liquid fire shrivels them up like a fly in a candle.[2]

After the ten-month-long battle at Verdun, which killed as many men as had the entire American Civil War, France's Gen. Henri-Philippe Pétain described surviving troops leaving the battlefield: "In their unsteady look one sensed visions of horror, while their step and bearing revealed utter despondency. They were crushed by horrifying memories." "Hell cannot be so terrible," another French soldier wrote. "Humanity is mad!"[3]

Elements of the 32d Division were sent into the madness on the front lines in the Alsace region, and to the far southern flank of the front. Finally, in late June, the entire 32d Division was lent to the French Sixth Army, fighting at the apex of the Marne salient. The Americans were ordered to a place called Château-Thierry.

The name became well known. Here the advance troops of the American army demonstrated their capacity to fight. The troops who broke the German lines during the next week were the 32d Division, followed by the 42d Division, which included among its senior leaders Col. Douglas MacArthur. That division already had a name, "Rainbow," because it had been formed of men from twenty-six states and the District of Columbia. The 32d was about to earn its own *nom de guerre*.

On August 6, troops of the 32d attacked German positions in and around the city of Fismes. The division fought with the French XXXVIII Corps, commanded by General de Mondesir, who went to the front to observe the new American troops in action. He saw them moving forward under heavy fire, overrunning German positions, decimating enemy machine-gun emplacements, and without hesitation moving on. *"Oui! Oui!"* the general exclaimed. *"Les soldats terrible, tres bien, tres bien!"*[4] General Charles Mangin, commander of the elite French Tenth Army, sent for the American 32d Division and put it alongside the shock troops of the French army — the Moroccan division which included the famous Foreign Legion. The 32d, now down to half its original strength, took and held the village of Juvigny, then participated in the Tenth Army's attack and breakthrough during the last days of August. In his official report, Mangin referred to the 32d as *Les Terribles*, and decorated the colors of all four regiments with the Croix de Guerre. In two months the division had fought eight German divisions, including the 4th Prussian Guards. But the war was not over.

In September, the 32d was brought back up to four-fifths strength and transferred to the American First Army. Through October, the 32d Division fought with the Rainbow Division and the 1st Division ("The Big Red One"). These troops broke the Hindenburg Line on October 14. The 32d Division had broken every German line it attacked from June through October of 1918. As a result, the division was assigned its distinctive insignia, a shoulder patch showing a red arrow cutting through a red line. The Wisconsin and Michigan men thus became the Red Arrow Division. Among the eighteen German divisions they had fought in whole or in part were the 3d, 4th, and 5th Prussian Guards, and the 28th ("Kaiser's Own"). A British historian describing American troops fighting the Prussian Guards in the towns of Seringes and Sergy, where the Guards fought to the last man, wrote, "The ruthless Prussians had met the remorseless men from young America."[5]

General MacArthur, whose division had fought beside the Red Arrow, was to remember those men from Michigan and Wisconsin. Twenty-four years later, in command of U.S. forces in the Southwest Pacific, he called on their sons.

MacArthur called on the 32d Division on 13 September, 1942, announcing that the Red Arrow would be sent to New Guinea. Americans did not yet know what jungle warfare was all about. If anything might have been worse than the war their fathers had fought, this war against Japan in the tropics was going to be it.

The 32d arrived on New Guinea inexperienced, unprepared, and ill-equipped. Their assignment was to move overland, through jungles and over fortified ridges, into murderous Japanese positions — without tanks or artillery, or even bazookas or flamethrowers — and take the strongpoint of Buna. Through malarial heat and humidity, the boys from the upper Midwest ran up against bunker after bunker from which the soldiers of Imperial Japan shot them down. The Americans wiped out the murderous emplacements one by one with small arms and grenades. What the Red Arrow learned, at great cost, the rest of the American army applied in the Pacific theater.

> To understand the 32nd, one must remember what it had gone through in its first weeks in Papau [New Guinea], and how quickly these men were riddled with malaria, dengue fever, tropical dysentery, and covered with jungle ulcers. Soon after he arrived at the front . . . [Lieutenant General Eichelberger] had the temperatures of the men of one company taken, and every member was running a fever.[6]

After nearly three months, the 32nd had lost nearly its whole original strength. Of the approximately eleven thousand men it had started with, 9,956 had been put out of action by the time Buna was taken. Fortunately, seven thousand of these men would have a chance of returning: they were down with malaria and other tropical illnesses. But seven hundred were dead and two thousand wounded. Lieutenant General Robert Eichelberger, in command of the campaign, wrote later:

> Buna was the first Allied Ground Force victory in the Pacific (the Buna Campaign was ended before the fall of Guadalcanal) and it was bought at a substantial price in deaths, wounds, disease, despair and human suffering. No one who fought there, however hard he tries, will ever

forget it. I am a reasonably unimaginative man, but Buna is still to me, in retrospect, a nightmare.[7]

Things did not get easier. The 32d was sent to the Philippines, landing on Luzon, the island that held Manila, the capital. The Red Arrow was ordered to open the Villa Verde Trail, a primitive route winding through jungle and over steep ridges, commanded by carefully fortified and sighted Japanese positions. The campaign would require 120 days of incessant combat.

The action of one platoon on February 23 and 24, 1945, serves to illustrate the fighting engaged in by the men of the Red Arrow. A Japanese emplacement on high ground had pinned down American forces for some days when nineteen men advanced up the hill. They surprised the thirty-one Japanese there, but the firefight that ensued lasted six hours. The Japanese were dug into holes as much as six feet deep, and were abundantly supplied with machine guns, mortars, grenades, and rifles. The Americans approached each hole, sometimes fighting hand to hand. The battle did not end until every Japanese soldier had been killed. During the night, a new Japanese force counterattacked the position, but was repulsed with "heavy casualties" by the platoon. According to the War Department, "This outstanding achievement by a platoon which consisted of only 19 men, in completely annihilating an enemy who outnumbered them and who had the advantage of both position and firepower, is in keeping with the finest traditions of American arms."[8]

The 32d Division fought an enemy characterized as "fanatical" because they refused to surrender. The sons of *Les Terribles* went after them in their caves, foxholes, dugouts — burning or asphyxiating them with flamethrowers, blowing them apart with grenades, sealing off their underground shelters with sandbags. The "cunning and determined enemy"[9] made the Americans pay. During the battle of annihilation that had been forced upon them, the 32d experienced "some of the bloodiest fighting in the history of the United States Army."[10] The division's 1st Battalion, 128th Infantry, replaced nearly all its personnel during this fighting, including six hundred killed. It killed fourteen hundred Japanese. A War Department citation, intending no irony, states this about the 3d Battalion, 128th Infantry:

> The fanatical enemy had to be killed to the last man, each determined to fight to the end. The onslaught of the American troops, closing from all sides, was so fierce that the spirit of the defenders of the Villa Verde Trail was broken forever. During the abovementioned period, the 3rd Battal-

ion killed at least 741 Japanese, while countless others were smothered and buried in caves. The indomitable courage of the 3rd Battalion, 128th Infantry Regiment, and their aggressiveness in battle against an enemy favored by both perfect defensive terrain and oriental fanaticism . . .[11]

In June, the 32d Division received a visit from the commander of the Army Ground Forces, Gen. Joseph "Vinegar Joe" Stilwell. Looking at the terrain the Red Arrow Division had fought through, he said, "Tough? This is as tough as anything could be. Terrain doesn't come any worse. . . . The division has a splendid record which will be very hard to beat."[12]

In sheer combat hours, their record was not beaten. The 32d was engaged for 13,030 hours, more than any other American division in the Second World War. General Tomoyuki Yamashita, commander of all Japanese forces in the Philippines, said in 1946 that the best troops he had faced were the men of the 32d Division — to whom he had personally surrendered on September 2, 1945.[13] During the four-month Luzon campaign, the division lost roughly eight thousand men, nearly five thousand to disease and the rest in battle. Sixty-seven hundred replacements arrived during that time. One of them, a Californian who arrived in early 1945, made the most eloquent statement about the 32d. In his reminiscences, Henry Brooks casually remarks: "32 Division is a Wisconsin, Michigan National Guard. I never met anyone from these states, they were all gone by the time I arrived."[14]

Many people have no idea that Americans fought in New Guinea during World War II. Someone once asked Dick Benson where he had fought first during the war. When he said "New Guinea," the questioner showed her surprise. Indignantly, with some irritation, Dick said simply, "That's where we licked the Japs." General Eichelberger put it another way: "at Buna they had won the Battle that started the infantry on the jungle road to Tokyo."[15]

But I never heard Dick speak about combat. None of his war stories mentioned flamethrowers in use, or caves being sealed, or "mopping up." I do not even know whether he was one of the few Wisconsin men who still answered roll call in August 1945, when the war ended. He was proud of his division, but he never spoke as though he were proud of himself. Whether he felt as decent as he always behaved, I never knew.

The heritage of the Iron Brigade, carried on in the world wars by the Red Arrow Division, is a glorious one in the written tradition of the U.S. Army. But it seems that the real war will never get in the books. The cause was a good one each time, and the men who fought for them have become our heroes, examples of unselfish decency. But the word "decency" is difficult to define in a world gone mad. These heroes of ours are also a little like ghosts. Their silences haunt us.

About thirty years after the war, Dick began to suffer from depression. A man who never complained, Dick did not talk about it much, but when he did to me — which was two or three times in the course of twenty years — he was angry and disgusted. He didn't have himself analyzed and he didn't relate his depression to the war. The local doctor and the VA gave him a prescription to try now and then, but nothing helped. It was just something he had to put up with, like the loss of part of his thumb to a circular saw. A guy learns to live with one thing and another. "But I sure as hell don't like it." That "damned depression" — something men of his era did not like to talk about by name — hit him off and on pretty hard and generally stayed with him at some level all the time.

He did not stop doing anything, but he acquired more of an edge. He objected to more things and got angry at more things — usually some new example, in his mind, of dishonesty, greed, cowardice, or other indecency. It would be little more than speculation to relate his psychology to the war; on the other hand, plenty of evidence taken from studies of veterans exists, suggesting that combat is responsible for mental troubles that emerge years and decades after a war. It is only reasonable to assume that Dick paid a price. A decent man seeing and doing the most indecent things imaginable is bound to be at war with himself.

We are the lucky ones if we did not have to fight a war to protect what we enjoy. Those others, from the Revolution on down, paid the price for us. In a country based in part upon the pursuit of happiness, it was a high price.

The question must be asked, even though no answer seems certain: Is fighting for any cause a decent thing to do — when you consider what warfare means? I assume that Dick thought absolutely No and absolutely Yes. In one sense, there are things you do not do no matter what. But warfare is one of those things that humanity has had to do, though it is the worst thing we do. If warfare ennobles some, it wholly debases others, according to Rufus Dawes of the 6th Wisconsin, Iron Brigade.

We have never figured this one out, and it is only half-bad that we have not. Had humankind ever decided once and for all that warfare is okay, even good, we would have wiped ourselves out before now: "It is well that war is so terrible, else we should grow too fond of it." Our doubts, reflected in the psychological price soldiers pay, have kept us alive as a species. On the other hand, we have never decided as a group that fighting back is wrong, despite the best efforts of our religions. These religions also tell us that something is wrong inside human beings. Many believe that from time to time we must resist that wrongness by force. We have never thoroughly tried the practice of loving our enemies, so we do not know whether or not such behavior would be the most practical of all solutions. "You first" has been the bottom line on this subject.

Meanwhile, the heathen rage. And decent men — dupes or heroes, who knows? — march off to defend their families. The other guy is always the heathen. And our job, as Gen. George Patton put it, is to make the other guy die for *his* country. From that standpoint, we all look pretty equal.

Dick might not have loved his war, but he did love his buddies. He stuck with the Veterans of Foreign Wars, and even accepted the unlikely position of chaplain of his post, because somebody had to do it. When he got together with his old messmates, it was the most raffish, good-hearted bunch of constant jokers you ever saw in your life; and when one of them died, all the rest turned out in uniform for the honor squad, and carried the casket, and knew and felt what the rest of us never will. You fought for your buddies, back then; you would give your life if you had to, not for your country or your politics, but for your messmates — and they would do the same for you. Warfare and horror and slaughter and honor had made a bond that nothing on earth could break.

One thing Dick would not have done, even for his friends, was to become something he detested. He would never have become a big shot by wheeling and dealing. He never would have made his way by stepping on other people. He would rather be poor than dishonest. He rejected what some of the people he defended are. He had his integrity. Oddly, in his integrity he accepted killing, while he would not accept greed or cheating.

Or did he? Was the man who helped "lick the Japs," as he phrased it, by shooting them to pieces the man Dick ever thought he would be, back on that farm in western Wisconsin? Who knows. Maybe he had grown up on tales of the World War heroics of Sergeant York — but of course he had no idea what it meant until he got there. Suppose he had known what it would take to become that man — would he have done it? If he had to, he probably would have. He went when they called him.

What did you have to do, I wonder, if you were an American soldier entering a Vietnamese village in 1968? What do you have to do if you are a young man or woman in an inner city today? What do you have to do to support your family? Maybe the ancient Greeks were right: tragedy is being forced into intolerable positions by powers greater than ourselves, and not knowing how to get out. What would we have to do to be decent people?

At the funeral today I looked toward the front pew where Mary sat, and next to her their son, Eric. They had lost their first child, Dick and Mary had, many years ago. Eric came along when Dick was fifty years old, and it was always a question as to whether Dick would live to see his son graduate from high school. But he did. The small boy I knew years ago sat there today, a big, strong fellow in his thirties, with children of his own. Eric is a decent man whom anyone would be proud to have as a friend. Dick felt like the luckiest man in the world to have such a son, and maybe he was. But I believe that it is all of us who are the lucky ones, because Dick defended us, and we knew him, and because, in the best way he could under the circumstances, he kept the faith.

Well, he was laid to rest this afternoon in the old cemetery where the Civil War soldiers lie, and a few remaining old friends fired blanks over his grave. We lucky ones stood by, flinched at the shots, then watched as the officer carefully took the folded flag and presented it to Mary, where she sat wiping her eyes. Somebody's darling was buried today. May he rest in peace.

NOTES

The Gettysburg Nobody Knows

1. Sickles later claimed credit for the Union victory at Gettysburg on the grounds that his corps absorbed and wore out Longstreet's attack. The claim makes sense until one realizes that it contains an unwarranted and insulting assumption: that the Army of the Potomac could not have held its original line against two Confederate divisions attacking across three-quarters of a mile of open fields.

2. Report of Brig. Gen. J. B. Kershaw, *The War of the Rebellion: A Compilation of the Official Records of the Union and Confederate Armies* (hereafter *OR*), ser. 1, vol. 44 (128 vols., Washington, D.C.: GPO, 1880–1901), 368.

3. Report of Lt. Col. Freeman McGilvery, *OR*, ser. 1, vol. 43, 882.

4. Gabor S. Boritt, ed., *The Gettysburg Nobody Knows* (New York: Oxford University Press, 1997).

5. William A. Frassanito, *Early Photography at Gettysburg* (Gettysburg: Thomas Publications, 1995), 325.

6. *Massachusetts Soldiers, Sailors, and Marines of the Civil War* (Boston: Adjutant General's Office, 1931).

7. Antoine de Saint-Exupery, *The Little Prince* (New York: Harcourt, Brace, and World, 1943), 87.

8. Mark Richardson and Richard Poirer, eds., *Robert Frost: Collected Poems, Prose, and Plays* (New York: Library of America, 1995), 275.

9. John 3:8 (KJV).

10. Ezekiel 37:1–8 (KJV).

Somebody's Darling

1. Michael Shaara, *The Killer Angels* (New York: Ballantine Books, 1974).

2. Glenn Tucker, *Lee and Longstreet at Gettysburg* (New York: Bobbs-Merrill, 1958).

3. Ps. 144:1 (paraphrased).

4. Emory M. Thomas, *Robert E. Lee: An Album* (New York: W. W. Norton, 2000).

5. Alan T. Nolan, *Lee Considered: General Robert E. Lee and Civil War History*

(Chapel Hill: University of North Carolina Press, 1991); Douglas Southall Freeman, *R. E. Lee: A Biography*, 4 vols. (New York: Charles Scribner's Sons, 1934–35).

6. Saint-Exupery, *Little Prince*, 87.

Ghosts of Gettysburg

1. Mark Nesbitt, *Ghosts of Gettysburg III* (Gettysburg: Thomas Publications, 1995), p. 27.

2. Ibid., pp. 15–17.

3. Ibid., pp. 33–34.

4. Ibid., p. 64.

5. Quoted in James M. McPherson, *Drawn with the Sword: Reflections on the American Civil War* (New York: Oxford University Press, 1996), p. 83.

A Ghost Story

1. Halldor Laxness, *Independent People*, trans. J. A. Thompson (New York: Vintage Books, 1997), p. 6

2. Ibid., p. 57.

3. Ibid., p. 279.

4. Ibid., p. 277.

5. Ibid., p. 35.

6. David Martin, *Gettysburg July 1*, Completely Revised Edition (Conshohocken, Pa.: Combined Books, 1995, 1996).

7. Henrik Ibsen, *Ghosts and Other Plays* (London: Penguin, 1964), p. 74.

8. Ibid., p. 61.

9. Ibid., p. 62.

10. *The Poems of Wilfred Owen*, ed. Jon Stallworthy (New York: W. W. Norton, 1985), p. 117.

11. Ibid., p. 192.

12. *Ghosts and Other Plays*, p. 73.

13. *Independent People*, 377–78.

14. Ibid., 379.

15. Ibid., 385–86.

16. Ibid., 386.

17. Ibid., 387.

18. Ps. 76:10a (KJV).

The American Iliad

1. All quotations are from Homer, *The Iliad*, trans. Robert Fagles (New York: Penguin, 1990).

2. Alan D. Gaff, *On Many A Bloody Field: Four Years in the Iron Brigade* (Bloomington: Indiana University Press, 1996), p. 189.

The Song of God

1. *The Bhagavad-Gita*, trans. Barbara Stoler Miller (New York: Bantam, 1986), p. 46.

2. McPherson, *Drawn with the Sword*, p. 243.

3. Homer, *Iliad*, pp. 570–71.

4. Donald Kagan, *On the Origins of War* (New York: Doubleday, 1995), p. 8.

5. *The Song of God: Bhagavad-Gita*, trans. Swami Prabhavananda and Christopher Isherwood (New York: Mentor, 1944), p. 39.

Wilderness

1. Quoted in Helen Addison Howard [no relation], *Saga of Chief Joseph* (Lincoln: University of Nebraska Press, 1941), p. 118.

2. Ibid., p. 350.

3. Ibid.

4. *In Pursuit of the Nez Perces: The Nez Perce War of 1877*, compiled by Linwood Laughy (Wrangell, Alaska: Mountain Meadow Press, 1993), p. 209.

5. J. F. C. Fuller, *Grant and Lee: A Study in Personality and Generalship* (Bloomington: Indiana University Press, 1957), p. 7.

6. Horace Porter, *Campaigning with Grant* (New York: Bantam, 1991), p. 65.

7. Ibid., 86.

8. Ibid., 175.

9. Bruce Catton, *Grant Takes Command* (Boston: Little, Brown, 1968), p. 124.

10. Edward Steere, *The Wilderness Campaign: The Meeting of Grant and Lee* (Mechanicsburg, Pa.: Stackpole Books, 1960), p. 422.

11. Ibid.

12. Ibid., p. 417.

13. Ibid., p. 441.

14. Gordon Rhea, *The Battle of the Wilderness, May 5–6, 1864* (Baton Rouge: Louisiana State University Press, 1994), p. 152.

15. Ibid., p. 153.

16. Ibid., p. 150.

17. Ibid., p. 147.

18. Quoted in Rhea, *Battle of the Wilderness*, p. 193.

19. Gaff, *On Many a Bloody Field*, p. 338.

20. Ibid.

21. Ibid.

22. Steere, *Wilderness Campaign*, pp. 365, 409.

23. Ibid., p. 351.

24. Robert Garth Scott, *Into the Wilderness with the Army of the Potomac* (Bloomington: Indiana University Press, 1985), p. 59.

25. Scott, *Into the Wilderness*, 60, 117, 127; Steere, *Wilderness Campaign*, 451.

26. Scott, *Into the Wilderness*, p. 127.

27. Sharon Eggleston Vipond, "A New Kind of Murder: The Iron Brigade in the Wilderness," unpublished manuscript, copy in author's possession, p. 21.

28. Vipond, "A New Kind of Murder," p. 23.

29. Porter, *Campaigning with Grant*, p. 206.

30. Ibid., p. 71.

31. Ibid., p. 73.

32. Catton, *Grant Takes Command*, p. 215.

33. Ibid., 95.

34. Stephen W. Sears, *Chancellorsville* (Boston: Houghton Mifflin, 1996), p. 432.

35. Porter, *Campaigning with Grant*, p. 88.

The Real War

1. James M. McPherson, *For Cause and Comrades: Why Men Fought in the Civil War* (New York: Oxford University Press, 1997), p. x.

2. Walt Whitman, *The Correspondence*, ed. Edwin Haviland Miller (New York: New York University Press, 1961), vol. 1, p. 216.

3. Ibid., p. 68.

4. Ibid., pp. 115–16.

5. Ibid., pp. 217–18.

6. Walter Lowenfels, *Walt Whitman's Civil War* (New York: Alfred A. Knopf, 1960), pp. 283–84.

7. Ibid., p. 14.

8. Ibid., 289.

9. Ibid., pp. 293–94.

10. Ibid., p. 294.

11. Ibid., p. 293.

12. Ibid., p. 283.

13. Walt Whitman, *Collected Poetry and Selected Prose* (New York: The Library of America, 1982), pp. 439–40.

14. Ibid., pp. 443, 445.

15. Ibid., pp. 450–51.

16. Ibid., pp. 425, 426.

17. Lowenfels, *Walt Whitman's Civil War*, p. 294.

"Nothing but Omnipotence"

1. *New York Times Review of Books*, Feb. 20, 1997, pp. 35ff.

2. Ibid., p. 36.

3. Ibid.

4. Ibid.

5. Ibid.

6. Ibid.

7. Ibid., pp. 36–37.

8. Ibid., p. 37.

9. Letter to author, Nov. 8, 1996.

10. Kagan, *On the Origins of War*, p. 8.

11. Letter to Albert G. Hodges, April 4, 1864, in Roy P. Basler, ed., *The Collected Works of Abraham Lincoln* (New Brunswick, N.J.: Rutgers University Press, 1953), p. 282.

12. Don E. Fehrenbacher, ed., *Abraham Lincoln: Speeches and Writings, 1859–1865* (New York: The Library of America, 1989), p. 359. Roy Basler, in *Collected Works of Abraham Lincoln*, tentatively dates the memorandum September 2, 1862 (emphasis in original).

A Soldier's Bones

1. Irwin Silber, ed., *Songs of the Civil War* (New York: Columbia University Press, 1960), 151–53.

Face-to-Face

1. Alan Nolan's phrase.

2. Archives, U.S. Army Military History Institute, Carlisle Barracks, Pa.

3. I Cor. 13:9,12 (KJV).

4. See Tony Horwitz, *Confederates in the Attic* (New York: Pantheon, 1998).

5. Silber, *Songs*, 134–35.

Witnesses

1. Horwitz, *Confederates in the Attic*.

2. Ibid., 376.

3. Ibid., 372.

4. M. L. Rosenthal, ed., *Selected Poems and Two Plays of William Butler Yeats* (New York: Collier Books, 1962), 93.

5. Yeats, "The Second Coming," ibid., 91.

Epilogue

1. This account is based upon Alan Nolan's *The Iron Brigade: A Military History* (Bloomington: Indiana University Press, 1961), 137–43; and Rufus Dawes's *Service with the Sixth Wisconsin Volunteers* (Dayton, Ohio: Morningside, 1984), 85–97.

2. Martin Gilbert, *The First World War: A Complete History* (New York: Henry Holt, 1994), 337–38.

3. Pétain quoted, ibid., 246; "mad," quoted ibid., 250.

4. www.e-2-127.org/history/ww1/32-ww1, p. 7.

5. Gilbert, *First World War*, 445. The Marines fighting in Belleau Wood lost 3,348 killed in action; their German opponents lost 8,624 (ibid., 435).

6. www.e-2-127.org/history/ww2/32ww2-3.html, p. 9.

7. www.e-2-127.org/history/ww2/32ww2-4.html, p. 4. (Data on same page.)

8. http://members.aol.com/Sarge000tb/32-ww2e.html, p. 5.

9. Ibid., p. 12.

10. Ibid., p. 13.

11. Ibid., p. 14.

12. Ibid., p. 16.

13. http://members.aol.com/Sarge000tb/32-ww2f.html, pp. 8,9.

14. www.angelfire.com/hi/RedArrowDivision/ww.2.html, p. 16.

15. http://members.aol.com/Sarge000tb/32-ww2f.html, p. 9.

Acknowledgments

References to the song "Somebody's Darling" (words by Marie Ravenal de la Coste) are from Irwin Silber, *Songs of the Civil War* (New York: Columbia University Press, 1960), pp. 145–47. The front quotation of Wilfred Owen is from *The Poems of Wilfred Owen*, edited by John Stallworthy (New York: W. W. Norton, 1986), p. 192. The J. Omar Good Fund and Visiting Distinguished Professorship provided money and opportunity to visit Civil War sites during the writing of parts of this book. I am grateful to Mary Brown, Lisa Crawford, Stephen C. Turner, Cara Lacy, Katie Frame, and Lynelle Gramm for their very helpful editorial readings. Thanks and apologies to Sarah McLachlan for the echoes from her song "Witness," on *Surfacing* (Arista Records, 1997). Thanks to Elizabeth for the pens and tuning, to Sarah for the reminder, and to Andrew for the happy book.

INDEX

 **Kent Gramm** is author of *Gettysburg: A Meditation on War and Values* and *November: Lincoln's Elegy at Gettysburg* and Program Director for the Seminary Ridge Foundation in Gettysburg. He has taught at colleges and universities in the United States and Germany.

DATE DUE